"...sure to become a classic.... His wording is concise, his explanations are insightful.... Whether you are new to astrology and want to delve further by yourself, or an astrologer who wants to add to your knowledge, this is the book for you."
    ---Aquarius Rising

"Simple and straight forward, his books have the writer's equivalent of nearly 'perfect pitch'."
    ---SSC Booknews

"This is the book you've been waiting for if you need guidance on chart interpretation..... Arroyo reminds us that the holistic approach is important to chart synthesis. ...gives new students and professionals a 'handle' to surmount some of the difficulties of chart interpretation."
    ---Astro News

"For the advanced, it's a quick reference book, and for students who tend to rely unthinkingly on interpretation paragraphs it will foster the ability to tune into an individual's character for themselves. Simplicity is the key: not to clutter an analysis with complex methods, minor factors and 'explanations' of every detail, but to concentrate on the unique inner dynamics of the person behind the chart... It is clearly laid out, well produced and easy to follow."
    ---The Astrological Journal (England)

D1293370

STEPHEN ARROYO is the author of numerous best-selling books on astrology, all of which have presented a type of astrology that is modern, innovative, and directed toward self-understanding. He is internationally renowned as a pioneer of in-depth astrology, which his writings express with remarkable clarity. His work is extremely popular around the world, with translations now appearing in nine languages. He has also been awarded the Astrology Prize by the British Astrological Association and the International Sun Award by the Fraternity of Canadian Astrologers. Mr. Arroyo holds an M.A. degree in psychology and for many years maintained a busy counseling practice. In addition, he taught some of the first credit classes in astrology in American colleges.

JERILYNN MARSHALL, the editor and research assistant for this book, holds a B.A. degree from Purdue and a Masters of Library Science from Vanderbilt University. She has been a student and practitioner of astrology since 1971. In addition to systematic research, she also made many significant creative contributions to the structure and content of this book. A specialist in all sorts of languages, she uses her Aquarian Sun energy to study not only the language of astrology, but also Russian, Italian, and others. She also served on the staff of two of the CRCS International Astrology Conferences.

Chart Interpretation
HANDBOOK

Guidelines for Understanding
the Essentials of the Birth Chart

STEPHEN ARROYO

Edited by Jerilynn Marshall

CRCS Publications
Post Office Box 1460
Sebastopol, California 95473

Library of Congress Cataloging-in-Publication Data

Arroyo, Stephen.
  Stephen Arroyo's chart interpretation handbook : guidelines for understanding the essentials of the birth chart / edited by Jerilynn Marshall.
    p.   cm.
  Includes bibliographical references.
  ISBN 0-916360-49-0 : $9.95
  1. Astrology.   I. Marshall, Jerilynn.   II. Title.   III. Title:
Chart interpretation handbook.
BF1708.1.A78   1989
133.5—dc20   89-9958
                                                            CIP

INTERNATIONAL STANDARD BOOK NUMBER: 0-916360-49-0

Published simultaneously in the United States and Canada by:
CRCS Publications
Distributed in the United States and internationally by
CRCS Publications
(Write for current list of worldwide distributors.)

Acknowledgments

I am especially indebted to Jerilynn Marshall for the tremendous amount of work she cheerfully did on this book. Without her remarkable efforts and abilities to tune in on the subtleties of meaning and language that I intended, not to mention her constant encouragement for over a year, this book could not have been created. Her innovative contributions far exceed what is usually implied by the term "editor." I am very grateful for her invaluable help on this project.

I am also deeply appreciative of the editorial refinements and insightful suggestions contributed by my long-time editor and friend, Barbara McEnerney, who has helped to give form to much of my writing for over a decade. Her intuition, deep knowledge of astrology, and refined discrimination have greatly added to the value of this book.

Finally, I would like to thank all the people who have strongly encouraged me to focus on writing once again, as well as all those who gave me critical and/or supportive suggestions regarding the form and content of this book. Special thanks go to Julie, Tony, and Mike.

Dedication

To Kathy, Julie, Opa, Nathan, and Kimberly, for making it possible for me to get away from the daily duties so I could again concentrate on writing.

CONTENTS

7. The Houses—Interpretive Guidelines   111

8. Understanding Planetary Aspects   131

9. Guidelines to Chart Synthesis   169

Introduction

We value things made by man but show scant respect for
what God himself has built.
　　　　—*Truth Eternal* by Master Charan Singh

Since the publication of my first books on astrology, I have continually received large amounts of mail from all over the world telling me how the material in the books is being used by students and practitioners of astrology, as well as by those who use astrology primarily as a self-help tool without any intention of becoming professional practitioners. Many people underline or annotate the books; others hand out photocopies of various sections to clients, students, or friends; and others tell me that an index or a further explanation of how to apply certain basic interpretive principles would be useful. However, until now I have not felt it necessary to provide additional material since I saw it as my primary role to outline as clearly as possible the basic principles and approach that I had discovered to be accurate and practical, a clarification that I felt was urgently needed if a true astrological psychology (or cosmic psychology) were going to be possible and soundly established.

In addition, I always felt that it was far preferable for students of astrology to learn to think for themselves—to think astrologi-

cally in relation to the *person* in question rather than to follow blindly traditional rigid rules of interpretation or to rely on the simplistic "interpretations" found in so many astrological cookbooks. I felt that it was important for students to make the extra effort to apply those guidelines and proven principles that I had already presented to specific cases and circumstances; and I felt that the considerable accuracy that could be achieved rather quickly would pleasantly surprise the student and lift him or her to a new level of understanding and competence. Furthermore, my books already contained many interpretive guidelines, examples, and case histories, far more in fact than one usually finds in astrological books where the lack of real life examples continually frustrates intelligent students of astrology as they attempt to master the basics of astrological understanding.

However, I have come to feel that a further development of the fundamental principles explored in my books, including more detailed interpretive guidelines, is in fact badly needed. What seems to me a substantial gap in the astrological literature is an explicit, concise compilation of interpretive guidelines that are easily accessible and usefully accurate both for students who are just learning to think astrologically, and for more advanced students, teachers, and practitioners who need a quick reference book. This book is an attempt to create an easily understood handbook that incorporates the widely-applicable meanings that emanate from the basic astrological factors. The purpose of this book is not only to make it easy to locate fundamental concepts and details of chart interpretation that are scattered throughout my books, but also to guide people in how to think astrologically, something a mere index cannot do. I also have kept the book focused on the *major* interpretive factors in any birth chart, excluding all those minor factors that so confuse beginning students and also often unnecessarily divert the attention of more experienced practitioners. I have also concentrated on understanding the natal birth chart only, preferring to explore the subject of transits and progressions in a separate volume.

This handbook is in many ways a sequel to and further development of the material presented in *Astrology, Psychology &*

The Four Elements and Astrology, Karma & Transformation, my first two books which have proven extremely popular and enduring world-wide. I am deeply indebted to those readers and teachers who continue to use and recommend my books, and I am grateful for their encouragement. This volume picks up where my earlier books leave off by showing how to combine and use principal keywords, concepts, and interpretive phrases, always keeping the emphasis on the *essential* meanings that "trip off" many related meanings and insights for the person using them.

In the design of this book, I was presented with a dilemma: I wanted to use extremely precise language for the interpretive guidelines, but also retain the wholistic, flexible, open-ended approach that had been so important and widely appreciated in my earlier works. The first word of this book's subtitle, *Guidelines*, is perhaps the central concept of this book. What is lacking in many astrology books are intelligent, linguistically accurate and precise *guidelines* with which to interpret the numerous details and the almost infinite combinations found in any birth chart. No wonder the new student of astrology gets confused, frustrated, discouraged, and often completely lost in the trivia that pervades most textbooks! What I have heard constantly for years from intelligent people trying to study and understand astrology on their own is that they simply don't relate to the neat paragraphs of "interpretations" that are supposed to apply to them. They naturally therefore question the accuracy and usefulness of astrology itself, instead of realizing that the book they are using is just one of many that purports to package up astrological "knowledge" for the general public but which fails to instill any real understanding or to convey any true insight that the individual will identify with and benefit from.

The modern trend of substituting quantity for quality is only too common in today's astrological cookbooks, and this baleful trend is even more evident in "computer astrology." The computerization of astrology that is spreading so rapidly today (primarily because it offers all sorts of people—astrologically qualified or completely unqualified—the chance to make more money more quickly) is bringing forth tremendous amounts of superficial, unfocused, completely useless "interpretations." In this type of automatically-produced astrological verbosity, no one ever bothers to define the words they use or to use words precisely or with nuances of subtler meanings. Using astrology for human benefit demands greater sophistication and more allowance for complexity than is evident in these odious misrepresentations of what astrology truly is.

Therefore, by focusing on precise, simple, in-depth language in this book, I'm certainly going against the grain of most astrological material being produced today, which seems lost in a profusion of words or minor astrological details or both. If the key concepts, phrases, and guidelines in this book are well chosen, they will penetrate to essential truths and insights that people can identify with and learn from. To what extent this attempt has succeeded, the reader will have to determine. But one thing about which I am confident is that this focus on the *essentials* of the birth chart is correct. It is correct because: (1) the essential factors are reliable, if properly understood; and (2) it is the fundamental major factors of a chart that most clearly reflect the fundamental major themes of the person's life. *Effective "chart interpretation" revolves around tuning into, understanding, and then illuminating the major life themes of the individual.* So many of the complex astrological methods and the minor astrological factors often promoted in books, lectures, articles, and mail-order computerized products will not reveal any new major theme in the person's life which the traditional factors and methods, *properly understood*, do not already clearly point to. As I have said in lectures to astrologers, if astrologers focus on trivia, they are trivializing astrology, and—I might add—giving astrologers an even more trivial image than they already suffer from in our society.

The following quotation from one of my lectures is worth repeating here as further explanation of why this new book must focus exclusively on the basic interpretive factors:

Rather than helping us to achieve chart synthesis and thus a *meaningful* evaluation of the person's major life themes, putting too many factors in a chart makes it harder to discriminate between the significant themes and the peripheral details. Since one can rationalize almost anything through a birth chart, and the more so the more points and methods and minor "planets" one uses, my view is that one should use a minimum of *major reliable* factors in order to see a client and his or her situation clearly. Otherwise, you'll project confusion, not order, to the client.

Just as air traffic controllers at an airport have difficulty distinguishing airplanes from other static on the radar screen and in distinguishing which is the closest approaching plane if there are too many in the sky at the same time, so astrologers using too many celestial factors will find it increasingly difficult to discriminate between the significant and the insignificant and so will more and more be inclined to impart confusion, illusion, and inaccurate observations to clients who are searching for clarity. People don't go to astrologers to find confusion or to collect a million petty details and speculations; they go to find some clarity and direction in their lives. Even if they want a prediction from you, that is their way of asking for clarity.

I mentioned above how important it is to the concept of this book that the keywords and interpretive guidelines be carefully chosen. I should probably briefly explain why such precision of language is so crucial. I have been concerned with achieving a precision of expression and a high level of reliability in astrological interpretation since 1967. The old black/white, good/bad, fortunate/unfortunate categories of old-fashioned astrology failed completely to give me the understanding or the reliability that I was looking for. As Harvard historian Dr. John King Fairbank stated, "It is not possible to think with critical power without being critical of the categories with which one is thinking." And yet, never at that time did I hear the fundamental assumptions and categories used by astrologers in their interpretive language questioned, challenged, or critically analyzed—until, that is, I encountered Dane Rudhyar's pioneering work.

Once the door to a new type of understanding of astrology was opened, it was only a matter of time and many, many dialogues with people about themselves and their charts before I concluded that astrology's greatest strength was in its description of the inner person: the primary motivations and needs, the inner situation at any given time, even the *quality* of the individual's consciousness—in short, the inner dynamics of the individual's entire physical and psychological energy field. Eventually, after years of experiment, vast reading in many fields, thousands of hours of counseling, and many kinds of research, it became obvious that astrology was essentially a language of experience and also—as I realized after years of study in the healing arts—a language of energy. I concluded that, for a truly *scientific* astrology (in the precise sense of the word), one must emphasize the inner dimensions of human life in order to achieve the level of accuracy that I sought.

The inner situation is actually more fundamental and thus more precisely symbolized by the astrological configurations than are outer circumstances. Once the inner essence manifests in the outer world, it fragments; the one becomes the many, and thus much more difficult to perceive in the limited number of factors in any chart. Hence, emphasizing exclusively outer events and circumstances, as so many astrologers do, ends up as a guessing game that is rarely successful. In my own search, once I found that one had to focus on the inner dimensions in order to find the characteristics that were *invariably* present when a certain planetary position or configuration occurred, it simply remained to experiment with many forms of verbal expression and many keywords and key phrases to see which were the most accurate and most effective at communicating subtle realities to clients. My first three books, and now this book, are the result of that quest. I hope the reader who uses this book will see these guidelines in this light, allow time to become familiar with them, and then ultimately feel free to pick and choose whichever parts of this book prove most useful.

Finally, as I mentioned above and focused on in my first book, *Astrology, Psychology & the Four Elements*, astrology is—perhaps preeminently—a language of energy. I know of no other such energetic language that rivals its accuracy, descriptive precision, and usefulness. What other language (or science, for that matter) can reveal the individual's primary *Voltage*, one's basic power and life force attunement, shown by the Sun? What other language can so precisely describe the individual's *Amperage*, one's rate of energy flow, shown by the Moon, or the individual's *Conductivity* or *Resistance*—in what way the life force can flow through the individual and into the world—symbolized by the Ascendant? These electrical analogies, developed by Dr. William Davidson, are just a fragment of the vast energy language of astrology.

If one is going to emphasize the energy approach to astrology and therefore the importance of the four elements, the following definitions—which I have used and found extremely accurate for many years—are worth keeping in mind as one studies the material in this book. These definitions also focus on astrology as a language of personal *experience*, as contrasted with the old-fashioned attempt to squeeze a description of outer events out of every astrological pattern.

The **ELEMENTS** are the *energy substance of experience.*

The **SIGNS** are the *primary energy patterns* and indicate specific *qualities of experience.*

The **PLANETS** *regulate energy flow* and represent the *dimensions of experience.*

The **HOUSES** represent the *fields of experience* wherein specific energies will be *most easily expressed* and *most directly encountered.*

The **ASPECTS** reveal the *dynamism and intensity of experience* as well as *how the energies within the individual interact.*

These five factors, defined and understood as stated above, constitute a remarkably comprehensive, sophisticated, and refined cosmic psychology; and any attempt to formulate a reliable science of astrology (or astrological psychology) must take into consideration the energy dimension of life that astrology maps and illuminates so explicitly. Practitioners in many traditions of the healing arts think and work in terms of "energy," and in fact quite a few are using or experimenting with astrology as a precise language of energy. So now it remains for the astrologers to realize what they have had all along and therefore to acknowledge astrology's energy dimension.

Unfortunately, many people actively involved with astrology today—both researchers and practitioners—are making the same mistake as have the materialistic scientists and most medical doctors today: namely, getting lost in details and hair-splitting analysis to the point of losing sight of the greater whole. The great wholistic truths of astrology easily become neglected and sometimes even derided when one becomes lost in technical details. Among these great truths are first, that Energy is the fundamental factor being analyzed and understood through astrology; and second, as a simple unifying factor, is the reality and importance of the traditional "four elements," still continually ignored or glossed over by most astrologers. And yet, the energies represented by the four elements are ultimately the fundamental realities of life that are being analyzed with astrology. In the energy approach, the elements are the active principles, and the planets primarily serve to activate and regulate those energies. In short, looking to the energy fundamentals of astrology will help all students and practitioners to be more realistic, accurate, and effective at communicating the great dynamic truths that astrology has to offer. Astrologers sometimes prefer to cling to the birth chart for security rather than to use it, put it aside, and then live courageously with that increased understanding. Astrology need not be a religion or the ultimate goal of a life's quest. It is more valuable as a stepping stone toward a greater understanding and a greater goal.

CHAPTER 1

ASTROLOGY AT THE THRESHOLD

The vast difference between astrology and other sciences, if I may put it thus, is that astrology deals not with facts but with profundities. The solid ground on which the scientist pretends to rest gives way, in astrology, to imponderables.

—Henry Miller

Especially for the benefit of new students of astrology, it seems advisable to discuss briefly some crucial issues that relate directly to the study and use of astrology in this era. In fact, it would be inappropriate for this book or any teacher of astrology to introduce people to the power and depth of astrological science without frankly discussing certain philosophical, scientific, and practical matters that have a direct bearing on anyone's attempt to use astrology in Western society today. I cannot begin to explore all the relevant issues in this handbook, and in fact I have devoted an entire book to these subjects (*The Practice & Profession of Astrology*), as well as a sizable section of another book (*The Jupiter/Saturn Conference Lectures: New Insights in Modern Astrology*, co-authored with Liz Greene). Therefore, the following thoughts must be regarded only as an introduction to a number of complex and controversial subjects.

Astrology is a unique subject in many ways, and its broad range of insight and application makes it sharply out of step with dominant trends of this materialistic age. It includes both science and art, both knowledge and wisdom, both inner life and outer life, and it is in fact based on the correlation of the cosmos with the individual (the ancient doctrine of the unity of macrocosm and microcosm—often expressed in the axiom "As above, so below"). This wholistic way of thinking sounds to most people today somewhat poetic and quaint at best, and ridiculous, naive, and superstitious at worst. The widespread prejudice against astrology in the Western world is, however, just one more example of the unthinking and actually unscientific skepticism expressed so automatically nowadays toward anything that acknowledges the reality of mind or spirit—the two most powerful fundamentals of human experience throughout history.

This skepticism and antagonism toward astrology is just a somewhat more forceful expression of the hostility that materialistic science and its short-sighted proponents and worshipers heap upon many branches of spiritual tradition, healing arts, philosophy, and the more ancient forms of psychology and personal guidance. Unfortunately, this unimaginative, narrow approach to human potential and to the central traditions of human thought has for some time dominated the major power centers of Western society, including the academic world which has the ethical obligation to preserve and study intellectual and cultural traditions and to emphasize the open-minded search for truth. A few people occasionally speak out against this trend of ignorance, such as the President of Yeshiva University, Norman Lamm, who wrote in 1987:

> . . . we must reassert the existence and value of the spirit . . . our society [must] learn that there is a larger wisdom that awaits our patient inquiry; that man is a spiritual as well as biochemical, psychological, political, social, legal and economic animal.

> An openness to spiritual dignity . . . means that the prevalent dogmas of scientific materialism and philosophical despair are not the only points of view worthy of scholarly attention; that belief in the reality of the mind and the existence of the soul does not condemn one as intellectually inferior and scientifically backward; . . . that knowledge ought to ripen into wisdom.

> (Excerpted from his address at the 100th anniversary of his University.)

The narrow attitude fostered by materialistic science—with its focus on the manipulation of nature—has tremendously inhibited many positive developments in society and has created the worldwide ecological disaster that we are only beginning to address. And yet, orthodox scientific work makes use of only one small part of the mind. By assuming that materialistic science is the only reliable road to knowledge and that only what can be scientifically shown to be valid is *real*, the Western world has effectively excluded the enormous dimensions of human life and experience which are inaccessible to the part of the mind employed in scientific analysis. Therefore, those who have experienced the value of astrology, rather than looking to orthodox science for "proof" and acceptance—which will never be forthcoming—would be using their energies more effectively by ensuring that their understanding of astrology (how it works best and what its appropriate scope and limitations are) is clear and reliable.

A study of the history of science, medicine, military strategy, politics, and many other fields of endeavor shows clearly that hardly an advance has escaped violent and fanatical opposition. For example, physicist Max Planck was so troubled by opposition to his ideas that he remarked that a "new scientific truth does not triumph by convincing its opponents and making them see the light, but rather because its opponents eventually die, and a new generation grows up that is familiar with it." (from "Planck's Principle," *Science*, 1978, by D. Hull, P. Tessner, & A. Diamond) I cannot help but recall what the maverick philosopher, poet, and artist William Blake wrote in this regard:

> He's a fool who wants a proof of what he can't perceive;
> And he's a blockhead who tries to make such a one believe.
> —The Marriage of Heaven and Hell

The reader may be thinking: "What has all this to do with astrology, which is certainly not a *new* idea?" Certainly, astrology is not a new idea in itself; but its use as a *modern* form of personal guidance and as a profoundly helpful tool in the helping professions does constitute a significant and radical advance. The reformulated, psychologically sophisticated type of modern astrology that has developed in the last fifty years *is* a new idea, a specific outgrowth in response to the desperate needs of Western society, and it has a great contribution to make in science, psychology, the healing arts, and in many other areas of endeavor. Dr. Carl Jung is often quoted as saying that astrology incorporates the sum total of the ancient world's psychological knowledge. This great reservoir of ancient wisdom and potential understanding of the mysteries of human life has now been studied anew in the light of modern psychology and other fields of knowledge, and it has been significantly reformulated by a few pioneers with a new language and with a myriad of new applications.

Astrology is now at the threshold of a *potential* major leap into a more significant place in modern life—**IF** it continues to develop in an intelligent way with modern language. Or it could revert to its previous fortune-telling and parlor-trick status, an image which unfortunately many practicing astrologers still seem to encourage by focusing on prediction of events—whether or not they call themselves "scientific astrologers" or similar more respectable names. Whether astrology crosses this threshold in the next two decades will depend more on the actions, competence, and professionalism of astrological practitioners and counselors than on the actions of astrology's powerful foes.

It has been publicized that very few of astrology's most vocal critics have the ethical and scientific integrity to have deeply researched the subject; generally, they have very little knowledge of its principles and virtually no knowledge of its practice. Their opinions, therefore, in the court of the science that they claim to represent must be regarded as worthless, no matter how loudly or dogmatically they are expressed. The followers of the chief traditions of Western astrology make certain definite statements concerning the expected significance of specific astrological placements, cycles, and configurations. Many, if not most, of these traditions are based on observations that have been repeated many times throughout the years. From the orthodox scientific viewpoint, only experiments that are equally numerous and which lead to quite different conclusions can be considered scientifically acceptable proof that certain specific astrological traditions are erroneous.

The real question here is quite simple and practical: are the statements of astrology justified? How can they be tested except by experiment? And what constitutes a valid, effective, and appropriate experiment for astrological principles? My conclusion, as I will explore below in more detail, is that only an experiential proof fits the need; and only experiments with living people in a clinical situation can fully show astrology's value and validity in its guidance, counseling, and psychotherapeutic applications.

One objection to astrology that is often heard from "scientists" who actually do not want to consider it remotely possible that astrology could be valid in *any* way is the idea that those who practice astrology cannot show any "cause and effect mechanism" whereby the planets could exert any "influence." Apart from the question of whether astrology should be considered only within a limited causal framework, the best refutation to this attempt to dismiss astrology is to explain that, as Dr. Jacob Zighelboim, M.D., Associate Professor at the UCLA School of Medicine stated in a lecture* I recently attended, throughout the history of science "the hardest thing to define is *mechanism*." All sorts of workable scientific principles and techniques and many kinds of medicines are employed routinely throughout the world without there being any understanding of *how* they work.

In the field of parapsychology, decades of research under stringent conditions and within the parameters of orthodox scientific experimentation has failed to explain the "mechanism" that may be associated with the various types of psychic phenomena. This experience in parapsychology research may well be regarded as an indication that the orthodox experimental approach may

---

*Lecture given at the conference "Homeopathy: Medicine for the 21st Century," San Mateo, California, April 29–May 1, 1988.

be completely inadequate for investigating astrology and other phenomena and techniques which work with the deeper reaches of the mind. Just because something is not readily measurable does not mean it does not exist and is not important!

The bulwark of materialistic science rests on statistics, measurement, and endless analysis of petty details, made all the more easy and voluminous today by widespread computerization. As one of the world's foremost experts on allergic diseases, Dr. Theron Randolph, M.D., writes: "Statistical methodology, computerization, and data retrieval systems favor analysis and fragmentation at the expense of synthesis and holism." (from "Bulletin of the Human Ecology Research Foundation") Dr. Randolph points out that these trends have made medicine and medical diagnosis more and more analytical, thus missing the larger picture of the patient's life situation. I feel this is a warning that should be heeded because similar trends currently happening in astrology also have the same limited results.

Statistical studies in astrology have been almost universally pointless. A few, like those done by Jeff Mayo correlating the Sun signs with extroversion or introversion and the well known Gauquelin studies over two decades that show definite patterns correlating planetary positions with various professions, have come up with positive results. But in general, as was pointed out in a recent book* showing the common failure of statistical studies to discover definite patterns that actually were present in the data, "If you do not know where to look for something, you will probably not find it." Hence, is it any wonder that those who know nothing of the intricacies and subtlety of astrology usually fail to discover significant results when they apply statistical approaches?

However, despite the limitations of the statistical approach in the investigation of subtle phenomena, statistically large numbers of clinical and experiential observations not only in astrology but also in the field of the natural healing arts are

---

*The January Effect, published by Dow-Jones Irwin, 1987.

often dismissed as "merely anecdotal," and thus not "reliable" information.

> According to critics of anecdotal information, what happens to a rat is scientific; what happens to a human is only anecdotal. How come? A rat cannot tell a scientist or a doctor what it feels. Its dead body tissue can only give evidence of what has happened to it. . . . With humans, what happens to their mind, feelings, and other perceptive organs is REAL and if one's telling of the experience is considered anecdotal, then that type of documentation should be acceptable. . . . Discrediting valid information as "anecdotal" is "unscientific." (from *Healthcare Rights Advocate*, Vol. II, Issue 2)

The great astrological writer and philosopher Dane Rudhyar clearly explained the dangers of astrology practitioners falling into the trap of imitating currently-fashionable "scientific" methods and standards:

> The present-day astrologer's concern about "raising" astrology to the acceptable level of a "science" by means of statistics and other analytical tools worshiped in our official "factories of knowledge" (universities) will not produce a more constructive approach to the problems faced by the astrological consultant in relation to clients. It is more likely to make such a relationship less effectual because, in order to be really effectual, it must be a relationship of person to person—and science does not deal with *individual cases*, but with *statistical averages*. Science does not deal with human values, but a person comes to an astrological consultant asking for help. He always unconsciously asks for help even if he is *consciously* motivated by curiosity. He comes for help with his sense of unique individual selfhood, even if his stated problem seems a common one; and it is with this sense of self that the consultant must deal. For we are all our own most basic problem; and astrology should help us meet it objectively and serenely. . . .
> (from *Astrology & the Modern Psyche*, 1977, page 182)

Actually, the philosophy and wholistic truths of astrology incorporate a worldview that is quite incompatible with the worldview of materialistic science, and anyone involved in astrological education, research, or promotion should be careful of trying to achieve a forced "integration" just for the sake of an illusory acceptance or coveted respectability. It would be far more fruitful to work hard to clarify astrology's unique strengths and to further define its principles and applications. An entirely pragmatic approach, evaluating results in people's lives and personal experience, is ultimately the only test that really matters in any healing art, helping profession, or psychological theory or method.

The Future of Astrology as a Science & a Profession

In what ways can astrology be considered a science?* In general, it can be designated a science simply because it comprises a set of principles and laws that have been accumulated through observation; and many of these principles can be tested and observed to be reliable. Just because one can find ideas and theories within the vast tradition of astrology that do not usually work and in fact some which are completely unreliable does not mean that a wholesale rejection of all astrological tradition is called for. Every science is constantly growing and changing, and the theories come and go, are discarded or refined, or are encompassed by a more complete theory; astrology is no exception. But the *fundamental principles* of astrology, if properly understood, are quite reliable.

Specifically, I believe that the *astrological psychology* that is currently available (although the serious student does have to search with considerable determination to find it) can reasonably be said to constitute a sort of cosmic psychology. This *Handbook* is in fact an attempt to set forth some of the fundamental principles and guidelines of this cosmic type of psychological science. When the astrological basics are interpreted with accurate, contemporary language and real understanding of what

---

*See also Arroyo's *The Practice & Profession of Astrology* for a more extensive discussion of the definition of science, how astrology is scientific, etc.

they signify in human psychology, they can then describe individual predispositions and illuminate the mystery of "human nature" far more than the constantly-changing theories, fads, and fashions of orthodox psychology.

Much of modern psychology has to rely on guesswork about people's drives and motives, and it usually attributes everything to an indecipherable mix of hypothetical "genetic and environmental factors." The resultant theories often are merely the projection of one person's individual viewpoint, experience, and prejudices. Astrology paints its pictures of human nature with much more varied colors on the vast canvas of the sky. A far broader range of human potentiality is thereby portrayed—and portrayed more clearly. Based on the observations of millions of people over long periods of time, astrology can legitimately claim to be a psychological science in the true sense of the word, when astrological fundamentals are properly understood and applied. And that proper understanding assumes that the areas of traditional application where astrology's reliability falls short are honestly recognized and fully acknowledged.

Ultimately, psychology needs a cosmic framework for dealing with the energy forces that enliven the child of the cosmos, which every human being is. By placing the human being in a cosmic frame of reference, astrology has a unique capacity for re-attuning a person's consciousness to his or her essential nature, and encouraging a depth of self-knowledge which is profound. No other theory or technique that I know of can illuminate human motivation or the *quality* of individual consciousness or experience so clearly, simply, and accurately. If astrology is utilized correctly, there need be no overlay of complex language or theory; it can just be *a simple explanation of cosmic factors and life energies operating within and through the individual.*

If astrology does indeed constitute such a profound and unequalled psychological science, the reader may then wonder how it can be introduced more effectively into society, a society where currently the role of "the astrologer" is one of no respect, constant ridicule, social ostracism, and little financial reward, except for a few media stars who sensationalize astrology for profit.

I have attempted to explore these questions at length in *The Practice & Profession of Astrology* and therefore refer the reader to that book for further discussion. However, one new idea not mentioned in that book is worth mentioning here, just in order to stimulate discussion among professionals or would-be professionals in the astrology field.

Apart from the individual's personal use of astrology for self-understanding and tuning into the rhythm of his or her life, I have for many years felt that astrology's greatest power and healing potential is experienced in the one-to-one counseling arts. There is no doubt in my mind that the level of accuracy and usefulness of astrological information is far greater in a dialogue situation than in a "reading" that may or may not have the person present. I wonder therefore if the future of astrology as a professional endeavor might not incorporate the title of "Astrological Counselor" or possibly even "Clinical Astrologer"? If any professional specialty like this would ever be established, it could only be done through the achievement of a clearly defined purpose, unified standards, and a high quality of practice. In short, a standard of excellence would have to be established, and quite demanding requirements accepted as the foundation for this new profession. This would of course take many years to achieve, and it would be slow to show results since the anti-astrology prejudice of the establishment is a powerful one. However, without a vocational opportunity for intelligent, capable people to practice an accepted profession and earn a reasonable livelihood, how will astrology ever attract and keep the kind of people who can make it prosper and grow and who can provide the kind of expert astrological services that the public has a right to expect?

CHAPTER 2
HOW TO USE THIS BOOK

Study the linked words, no doubt, but look
Behind them to the action that they indicate;
And having found it, throw the words away
As chaff when you have sifted out the grain.
Study the (spiritual) sciences, master their inner meaning;
Then, having done so, discard the books.
                                                —Upanishad

This book does not attempt to sum up all possible meanings of the primary factors found in a birth chart. Nor does it purport to convey to the reader instant "knowledge" or sensational statements that will impress others. Astrology's greatest strengths are squandered by pandering to a public and media that craves a type of sensationalism that is not the proper product of this subtle and profound science. This book will encourage understanding in direct proportion to the reader's effort at concentration and deep reflection. It is a book for the practical interpretation of birth charts, supplying the practitioner, teacher, or student with interpretive guidelines that he or she can adapt, elaborate upon, and use to elicit further meaning in the context of the chart, person, and situation being considered.

The crucial word is *guidelines*. Guidelines are meant to be used in order to get somewhere, and—in the case of this book—to gain deeper understanding of particular charts and people and eventually of astrology itself. Those who use this book only passively will not derive its full value; but those who use the guidelines as *springboards* for personal reflection and—in a consultation—for a dialogue that centers on the deeper reality, feelings, and inner experience of the other person, will, I feel, find this book quite valuable. Using this book as a way to tune in, or help others tune in, to the deeper self, to the subtle feelings and rhythms and needs that are so often ignored, will enable the reader to develop a personal method of astrology that focuses on meaning and purpose in life. That sort of astrology is far more profound, useful, and accurate than the verbose descriptive material of most books and computer programs that merely glance over the surface, leaving the individual essentially unaffected and indifferent.

As mentioned previously, one must focus on inner experience in astrological work to achieve a high level of accuracy. I would especially caution the newer student not to assume that astrology will be capable of "explaining" *everything*, just because it is a type of cosmic science. This erroneous assumption is all too common among practicing astrologers and new students of astrology who are ablaze with enthusiasm. The belief that astrology has infinite applications and that its accuracy is invariably high in all these applications has many unfortunate effects, some of which I have explained in other books. One harmful result that is quite evident in recent years is that astrologers are tempted to fill in the apparent gaps by adding more and more factors to the birth chart, hoping, I assume, eventually to be able to "account for" or "explain" virtually every petty detail of life. This of course is a futile effort. Life is an infinitely varying dance of energy, and the mysteries of life, the Self, and the human Soul will always transcend all mental approaches and techniques. This is all the more reason why I refer to the essential building blocks of this volume merely as *guidelines*; they can be used only for guidance in seeking greater understanding of self and others. It cannot be claimed that these guidelines or any other chart interpretation materials are the "last word" or constitute "complete" interpretations. Nothing in human life is ever "complete"; everything is always changing and transforming.

As mentioned above, one should not assume that astrology will "explain" everything. One must turn to religion, philosophy, or mysticism for ultimate explanations. Astrology, although not as great an *explainer* as many would like to believe, is a great *illuminator*. It shines a light where before there was darkness and confusion. But astrology can illuminate only if the astrologer is capable of focusing that light! Otherwise, the light is scattered and thus diffuse and faint. The brilliant light of understanding that the remarkable symbols of this cosmic language can reflect can easily be distorted or lost if the person using astrology is not a clear, sharp lens. And that is the purpose of these guidelines—to help the individual to *focus* on the *essential* meanings and thus to be a clear lens for illuminating the complexities and dark corners of life and human nature.

In this book, I have assumed that the reader is familiar with the basic factors of traditional astrology at least to some extent. Therefore, I have not repeated what is readily available in dozens of other basic texts. I am also assuming that the reader has a birth chart and at least fundamentally knows how to ascertain the sign and house positions of the planets. For those who do not have such a chart, I recommend that they write the following company to order a "basic natal chart" for a cost of under $5: ACS, P. O. Box 16430, San Diego, CA 92116. It is essential that one send in the most accurate birth time available, as well as the birth date and place. Better still for absolute beginners would be to have a knowledgeable person explain to them the essential major components of their birth charts. In addition to reading as widely as possible in the literature of astrology,* I would also recommend

---

*Although perhaps the most important guideline regarding which books to read is that one should find writers who "speak your language," the reader would be well advised to read at least some works by such giants of astrology as Dane Rudhyar, Margaret Hone, and Charles Carter, as well as various works by the modern writers who specialize in astrological psychology in a modern language. The reader is encouraged to read the other books by Stephen Arroyo, which complement this work. Beginners are especially referred to his *Astrology, Psychology & the Four Elements* for more details on many of the basics of astrology as a language of energy and the rationale for this approach. There are so many astrological books that are worth studying, they cannot all be mentioned here. The reader should consult the "Suggested Readings" list in Arroyo's *Astrology, Karma & Transformation*. *Astrology: The Divine Science* by Marcia Moore & Mark Douglas is especially recommended. It is very difficult to find, so readers are advised to write CRCS Publications for information on obtaining copies. (See address on title page.)

that newer students begin to do as many charts as possible, talking with the other person in detail in a free-ranging dialogue, making frequent use of the guidelines in this book, and never hesitating to acknowledge frankly any confusion, ignorance, or lack of understanding. It is only through an honest trial-and-error experimentation with astrology with large numbers of people that the language of astrology completely comes alive. This kind of dialogue is a joint exploration of the issues that face the person, the person's deeper character and motivations, and what light astrology can throw on these subjects.

It is also important to note that, in order to use this book most effectively, one should open-mindedly consider the accuracy of *all* the interpretive phrases, whether they may seem positive or negative. [The function of the astrological practitioner, after all, is not to flatter the client with endless complimentary statements!] Those readers who have studied many different astrology texts will have noticed that many astrological writers fall into the trap of making ''either/or'' statements. It is easier to think and write that way than to deal with the complexities and nuances of life, and it is a temptation that is hard to resist as a writer attempts to organize astrological data into accessible categories. I have fallen into this trap more than once in my own writings. If life were only that simple, practicing and understanding astrology would also be much simpler.

In fact, however, positive and negative often manifest together in life, alternating or weaving together in the fabric of each individual personality in such a unique way that we have great difficulty in trying to unwind all the strands to facilitate simple analysis. It is realistic to assume that most people have a broad combination of ''positive'' and ''negative'' traits, tendencies, and motives. And, in many ways, what may seem a ''negative'' trait to one person may be quite an admirable quality to another. One person may despise the impatience and abrasiveness of an Aries, for example, while another person may deeply appreciate the action-oriented personality and honest bluntness of the Aries. In other words, in spite of the impression given by the pat interpretations of so many ''cookbooks,'' astrology is not an *either/or* sort of study, founded on simple black and white judgments. It is a subtle science of energy that encompasses an infinite variety of shadings and combinations. Unlike typical "theories of personality" in orthodox psychology, it includes innumerable nuances of personality, character, and creative potential. As psychologist Dr. Ralph Metzner has written,

> As a psychologist and psychotherapist, I have been interested in another aspect of this baffling and fascinating subject. We have here a psychological typology and diagnostic assessment device far exceeding in complexity and sophistication of analysis any existing system. . . . the framework of analysis—the three interlocking symbolic alphabets of zodiac "signs," "houses," and "planetary aspects"—is probably better adapted to the complex varieties of human natures than existing systems of types, traits, motives, needs, factors, or scales.
>
> (*Astrology: Potential Science & Intuitive Art* from *The Journal of Astrological Studies*, 1970)

The newer student of astrology often becomes bewildered by the vast number of interpretive options that even a basic birth chart presents. Such questions as "What do I *focus* on?" and "What do I emphasize within the limited time period of a consultation?" are important and must be answered. And yet, the literature of astrology provides little guidance in this area* and only scattered answers to such questions. I have attempted to provide some clarification to these issues in a number of my books, and in this volume have decided to make the structure of the book itself reflect the relative importance of the various factors that constitute a basic birth chart.

Perhaps most important is the emphasis placed in this book on the four elements as the basic energies analyzed by astrology and on the element and sign placements of the "personal" planets. The outer planets (Uranus, Neptune, and Pluto) have not been emphasized except where they have a powerful impact on the individual, e.g., their aspects to the personal planets and their house placements. I have seen far too many beginning

---

*Tracy Marks' *The Art of Chart Interpretation* is one of the few books that emphasizes how to discriminate between the most important chart factors and those that are secondary. (Available from the publisher of this book.)

students overemphasizing a sign position of Uranus, for example, or even more often an aspect between two of the outer planets, not knowing that everyone born for a number of years shares that same configuration because of the slow movement of the outer planets. Hence, there can be little *individual* impact of that factor, except insofar as it aligns with the "personal planets" or Ascendant. So, when defining precise guidelines to utilizing and understanding the *essentials* of the birth chart, there is no reason even to include such details. Anyone using astrology should invariably focus on the five personal planets (Sun, Moon, Mercury, Venus, and Mars), as well as the Ascendant point, and then on anything that colors or modifies those primary factors.

If, for example, Neptune conjuncts the Ascendant or its opposite point, the Descendant, then Neptune becomes an important factor in the personality and the energy field, not because of its sign position—but *because of how it ties in to the primary focal points and structures of the chart.* If, for another example, Uranus or Pluto *closely* aspects the Sun, that person would then have a strongly Uranian or Plutonian attunement and consciousness, not because of the sign positions of those distant planets, but because of the intensity of vibration set up by the closeness of the angle between the Sun and the outer planet.

Therefore, in line with the importance of the personal planets, the largest section of this book gives numerous guidelines for understanding those planets' sign positions, as well as the sign positions of Saturn and Jupiter. In order to keep the focus on the energy approach to astrology, simple guidelines for the elements of the signs and for the element positions of the planets are also provided. With this material on the elements and the planets-in-signs guidelines alone, one could do quite amazing astrological work, with impressive accuracy.

Next in importance is the Ascendant, but instead of simply listing keywords similar to those of the Sun in the signs so that each rising sign could be described, I decided to address a common point of perplexity for newer students of astrology: distinguishing between a sign's manifestation as a Sun sign and how it appears when it is rising. Far more could be said to differentiate between each pair (for example, between Taurus Ascendant and Taurus Sun), but in a book of concise guidelines, it seems enough to acknowledge the difference and to point toward some obvious contrasts I have observed over the years.

In the section on houses, I decided to focus on the wholistic principles from which all specific house interpretations can be derived and on numerous guideline phrases designed so the practitioner can "plug in" the specifics of a given chart and then use the resulting combination as a springboard for personal reflection or dialogue. In other words, in the section on houses I want to encourage students to think for themselves and to explore the myriad possibilities of *inner and outer life* that a particular planet/house combination can symbolize.

In the aspects section, the emphasis is placed on the *planets* in specific angular relationships, rather than on what the exact angle is. The habit in traditional astrology of grouping all squares together, all trines together, etc., contributes to perpetuating the erroneous notion that all squares are "bad" or "difficult," that all trines are "good" or "easy," and so on. This habit persists, often as an undercurrent, in the thinking even of those who consciously claim to have outgrown that limiting old way of seeing aspects. Of far more importance, however, are the *planets* involved in an aspect, how well they *blend together* and function in the signs occupied, and how a particular aspect is integrated into the structure of the chart as a whole.

As further guidance for those who ask "What do I focus on?", I should also repeat the advice I have given many students: Even if you feel that you understand only a small part of a chart, follow what you *do* understand and it will lead you into the structure and major themes of the rest of the chart. And don't worry about doing a "complete chart interpretation," for it is impossible. Instead of getting lost in the endless details of a *chart*, it is better to focus on what is *important* in the person's nature and life and on what kind of person he or she is. Since the birth chart is fully realized only in the living human being, a "complete chart interpretation" is achieved only insofar as the fabric and intricacies of the individual's whole life and personality are revealed, better understood, and more fully accepted.

Finally, astrology can only be *taught* up to a certain point. It is of course important that one learn the best type of astrological science available in order to do precise and helpful work, but after fundamentals, philosophy, and reliable interpretive principles are learned, it is then the astrologer that matters more than the astrology. The application of the science is an art and requires the subtlety of an artist. The question thus becomes: What kind of an artist are you? Are you a clear lens through which the cosmic factors can be clearly reflected and focused? One's own personal development, beliefs, ideals, and sensitivity are therefore crucial in determining how effective and beneficial any individual's astrological art becomes.

It is still true that the specific kind of astrological theory you embrace *is* important (contrary to what some "open-minded" astrologers believe). As Einstein said, "It is theory that decides what we can observe." Defining one's astrological philosophy and fundamental theory and approach is therefore imperative to achieve a clear perspective and solid grounding in astrological work.

But the level of personal development you have achieved is at least as important, in the way it enables you to understand life and human beings. After all, the intellect can only function within the scope allowed by the person's level of consciousness (or level of soul development, one might say). It is therefore to one's inner life and inner development that one must ultimately look, not only as the only way toward a refined understanding and effective use of astrology, but as the only way toward an evolving way of being.

Key Concepts & Definitions

A key to the understanding of all astrology is within the reach of anyone who truly understands the meaning of the following definitions:

The **ELEMENTS** are the *energy substance of experience.*

The **SIGNS** are the *primary energy patterns* and indicate specific *qualities of experience.*

The **PLANETS** *regulate energy flow* and represent the *dimensions of experience.*

The **HOUSES** represent the *fields of* experience wherein specific energies will be *most easily expressed* and *most directly encountered.*

The **ASPECTS** reveal the *dynamism and intensity of experience* as well as *how the energies within the individual interact.*

These five factors comprise a comprehensive cosmic psychology, and it is the art of combining them that results in the language of energy called astrology.

These factors are combined in the following way: A particular dimension of experience (indicated by a certain planet) will invariably be colored by the quality of the sign wherein it is placed in the individual's chart. This combination results in a specific urge toward self-expression and a particular need for fulfillment being defined. The individual will confront that dimension of life most immediately in the field of experience indicated by the planet's house position. And, although the urge to express or to fulfill that dimension of experience will be present in anyone having a certain planet-sign combination, the specific aspects to that planet reveal how easily and harmoniously the person can express that urge or fulfill that need.

CHAPTER 3

THE FOUR ELEMENTS & THE TWELVE SIGNS

The "four elements" of astrological tradition refer to the vital forces (or energies) that make up the entire creation that is commonly perceived by human beings. The four elements in a birth chart reveal the ability to participate in certain realms of being and to tune in to specific fields of life experience. These elements have nothing to do with the elements of chemistry and in fact transcend them completely. The astrological birth chart is drawn for the moment of first breath, that instant when we immediately establish our lifelong attunement with cosmic energy sources. The birth chart therefore reveals your energy pattern or cosmic attunement to the four elements. In other words, the chart symbolizes the pattern of the various vibratory manifestations that comprise the individual's expression in this plane of creation.

The four elements—*Fire, Earth, Air,* and *Water*—each represent a basic kind of energy and consciousness that operates within everyone. Each person is consciously more attuned to some types of energy than others. Each of the four elements manifests in three vibrational modalities: *Cardinal, Fixed,* and *Mutable.* Combining the four elements with the three modalities produces the *twelve primary patterns of* energy called the Signs of the Zodiac.

One way of understanding these various energy patterns is to analyze them in terms of their modalities. The *Cardinal Signs* correlate with the principle of *action* and symbolize *initiating movements of energy in a definite direction.* The *Fixed Signs* represent *concentrated energy gathered inward toward a center or radiating outward from a center.* The *Mutable Signs* are correlated with *flexibility* and *constant change* and may be conceived as *spiralic patterns of energy.*

The element of any sign that is emphasized in a chart (by significant planetary placement in that sign)* shows a specific type of consciousness and method of perception to which the individual is strongly attuned.

Air Signs are correlated with the mind's sensation, perception, and expression, especially related to personal interaction and to geometrical thought forms and abstract ideas.

Fire Signs express the warming, radiating, energizing life principle which can manifest as enthusiasm, faith, encouragement, and the drive to express self.

Water Signs symbolize the cooling, healing principle of sensitivity, feeling response, and empathy with others.

Earth Signs reveal an attunement with the world of physical forms and a practical ability to utilize and improve the material world.

The elements have traditionally been divided into two groups, *Fire* and *Air* being considered active and *self-expressive,*

---

*See Chapters 11, 12, and 14 of Astrology, Psychology & the Four Elements for a comprehensive discussion of how to understand and "measure" which elements are emphasized in any chart. Especially Chapter 12 should be consulted to understand how to evaluate the relative strength of the four elements in a particular birth chart.

and *Water* and *Earth* considered passive, receptive, and *self-containing*. This differentiation is of great importance in a wholistic approach to birth charts. These terms refer to *the mode of operation of these energies* and to the individual's method of self-expression rather than to a generalized quality that can be haphazardly and rigidly applied to all people in a certain category.

For example, the Water and Earth signs are more self-contained than the Fire and Air signs in that they live more within themselves and don't allow themselves to project their essential energy outwardly without a good deal of caution and forethought. However, this enables them to build a solid foundation for action. The Fire and Air signs are more self-expressive since they are always ''getting it out,'' pouring forth their energies and life-substance unreservedly (at times ignoring limits completely): the Fire signs by direct action and the Air signs by social interaction and verbal expression. This classification of elements, and the fact that the signs of the same element (e.g., Aries, Leo, and Sagittarius—all Fire) and of the elements in the same group (e.g., Taurus & Pisces = Earth & Water) are considered to be generally ''compatible,'' is of the greatest importance not only in the interpretation of individual charts but also in the art of chart comparison.

Each sign of a specific element is a different mode of expression of the same elemental energy and represents a different level of development and pattern of energy.

THE FIRE SIGNS: Aries, Leo & Sagittarius

The Fire signs express a universal radiant energy, an energy which is excitable, enthusiastic, and which through its light brings color to the world. The Fire signs exemplify high spirits, great faith in themselves, unending strength, and a direct honesty.

KEY CONCEPT:	CHARACTERISTICS &
Radiant energy, confidence, & initiative	KEY WORDS:

fearless impulsiveness
high spirits
enthusiasm
strength
direct honesty, even bluntness
outgoing
freedom of expression
directed willpower &
  leadership
demonstrative
impatient

THE AIR SIGNS: Gemini, Libra & Aquarius

The Air signs express the life-energy which has been associated with breath or what the yogis term "prana." The Air realm is the world of archetypal ideas beyond the veil of the physical world; in the air element, the cosmic energy is actualized into specific patterns of thought. The Air signs have the inner need to detach themselves from the immediate experiences of daily life, and thus to gain objectivity, perspective, and a rational, reflective approach to everything they do.

KEY CONCEPT:	CHARACTERISTICS &
Mental sensation, perception, & expression	KEY WORDS:

living through the mind
visualization
rationalization
detachment & perspective
craving for understanding
verbalization
need for relationship &
  sociability
communicative & curious
awareness of others as
  individuals
concepts & principles

THE WATER SIGNS: Cancer, Scorpio & Pisces

The Water signs are in touch with their feelings, in tune with nuances and subtleties that many others don't even notice. The Water element represents the realm of deep emotion and feeling responses, ranging from compulsive passions to overwhelming fears to an all-encompassing acceptance and love of creation. The Water signs know instinctively that to realize their soul's deepest yearnings, they must protect themselves from outside influences in order to assure themselves the inner calm necessary for deep reflection and subtlety of perception.

KEY CONCEPT:
Deep emotion, empathy
& feeling response

CHARACTERISTICS &
KEY WORDS:
sensitivity
realizes the reality of the
    unconscious and/or
    unconscious of reality
intuition
purification & purgation
psychic sensitivity
deep reflection
habitual secrecy & need for
    privacy
ability for compassionate
    service
need for emotional
    involvement with others

THE EARTH SIGNS: Taurus, Virgo & Capricorn

The Earth signs rely heavily on their senses and practical reason. Their innate understanding of how the material world functions gives the Earth signs more patience and self-discipline than other signs. The Earth element tends to be cautious, premeditative, rather conventional, and usually dependable. Knowing their niche in the world is especially important to the Earth signs, for security remains a constant goal for them throughout their lives.

KEY CONCEPTS:
Practical ability to utilize
the material world

CHARACTERISTICS &
KEY WORDS:
attunement to physical world
heightened physical senses
practicality
patience
self-discipline
persistence
cautiousness
dependable
premeditative
conventional

Please refer to the first two pages of Chapter 5 for more details
on each individual sign, and how they are differentiated from
each other.

CHAPTER 4

THE PLANETS

Key Concepts for the Planets

	Principle	Urges Represented	Needs Symbolized
SUN:	Vitality; sense of individuality; creative energy, radiant inner self (attunement of soul); *essential* values	Urge to be and to create	Need to be recognized and to express self
MOON:	Reaction; sub-conscious predisposition; feeling about self (self-image); conditioned responses	Urge to feel inner support; domestic and emotional security urge	Need for emotional tranquility and sense of belonging; need to feel right about self
MERCURY:	Communication; conscious mind (i.e, logical or rational mind)	Urge to express one's perceptions and intelligence through skill or speech	Need to establish connections with others; need to learn
VENUS:	Emotionally-colored tastes; values; exchange of energy with others through giving of self and receiving from others; sharing	Social and love urge; urge to express affections; urge for pleasure	Need to feel close to another; need to feel comfort and harmony; need to give of self's emotions
MARS:	Desire; will toward action; initiative; physical energy; drive	Self-assertive and aggressive urge; sex urge; urge to act decisively	Need to achieve desires; need for physical and sexual excitement
JUPITER:	Expansion; grace	Urge toward a larger order or to connect self with something greater than self	Need for faith, trust, and confidence in life and self; need to improve self

	Principle	Urges Represented	Needs Symbolized
SATURN:	Contraction; effort	Urge to defend self's structure and integrity; urge toward safety and security through tangible achievement	Need for social approval; need to rely on one's own resources and work
URANUS:	Individualistic freedom; freedom *of* ego-self	Urge toward differentiation, originality, and independence from tradition	Need for change, excitement and expression without restraint
NEPTUNE:	Transcendent freedom; unification; freedom *from* ego-self	Urge to escape from the limitations of one's self and of the material world	Need to experience a oneness with life, a complete merger with the whole
PLUTO:	Transformation; transmutation; elimination	Urge toward total rebirth; urge to penetrate to the core of experience	Need to refine self; need to let go of the old through pain

Positive-Negative Expression
of Planetary Principles

Each planetary principle can be expressed positively and crea-tively or negatively and self-destructively. In other words, one's attunement to each dimension of experience may be in harmony with higher law or in a state of disharmony and discord. This results in the creative use or in the misuse of these various ener-gies, forces, and attunements. The aspects to each planet must be analyzed in order to understand the degree of harmony or discord present within the individual.

	Positive Expression	*Negative Expression*
SUN:	Radiation of spirit; creative and loving pouring forth of self	Pride; arrogance; excessive desire to be special
MOON:	Responsiveness; inner con-tentment; flowing, adapt-able sense of self	Oversensitivity; insecurity; inaccurate, inhibiting sense of self
MERCURY:	Creative use of skill or intelligence; reason and power of discrimination used to serve higher ideals; ability to come to agree-ment through objective under-standing and clear verbal expression	Misuse of skill or intelli-gence; amorality through rationalization of anything; opinionated and one-sided "communication"
VENUS:	Love; give and take with others; sharing; generosity of spirit	Self-indulgence; greed; emotional demands; inhibition of affections

	Positive Expression	*Negative Expression*
MARS:	Courage; initiative; will-power consciously directed toward legitimate aim	Impatience; willfulness; violence; improper use of force or threats
JUPITER:	Faith; reliance on higher power or greater plan; openness to grace; optimism; openness to self's need for improvement	Over-confidence; laziness; scattering energy; leaving the work to others; irresponsibility; over-extending self or promising too much
SATURN:	Disciplined effort; acceptance of duties and responsibilities; patience; organization; reliability	Self-restriction through too much reliance on self and lack of faith; rigidity; coldness; defensivenes; crippling inhibition, fearfulness, and negativity
URANUS:	Attunement to truth; originality; inventiveness; directed experimentation; respect for freedom	Willfulness; restless impatience; constant need for excitement and purposeless change; rebellion; extremism
NEPTUNE:	Attunement with the whole; realization of spiritual dimension of experience; all-encompassing compassion; living an ideal	Self-destructive escapism; evasion of responsibilities and self's deepest needs; refusal to face one's motives and to commit self to anything
PLUTO:	Acceptance of the need to focus one's mind and will power on one's own transformation; having the courage to face one's deepest desires and compulsions and to transmute them through effort and intensity of experience	Compulsive expression of subconscious cravings; willful manipulation of others to serve one's own ends; ruthlessly using any means to avoid the pain of facing one's self; infatuation with power

The Planets in the Elements

The Sun

The Sun sign's element is usually dominant in considering the overall psychology of a person. This is so because the Sun sign's element reveals the attunement of one's basic vitality, identity, and power of self-projection, as well as the fundamental quality of his or her consciousness. It also shows what is "real" to the individual, for it is the unconscious assumption of what is particularly real and what isn't that determines how the person will focus his or her energy.*

For example, the *Air Signs (Gemini, Libra & Aquarius)* live in the abstract realm of thought, and a thought for them is as real as any material object. The *Water Signs (Cancer, Scorpio & Pisces)* live in their feelings, and it is their emotional state that determines their behavior more than anything else. The *Fire Signs (Aries, Leo & Sagittarius)* live in a state of highly excited, inspired activity, and maintaining that state of being is crucial for the fire signs to stay healthy and happy. The *Earth Signs (Taurus, Virgo, & Capricorn)* are grounded in physical reality; the material world and considerations related to security and achievement motivate their behavior more than anything else.

The element of one's Sun sign reveals the basic inner force motivating everything we do. The element of the Sun sign also gives insight into how any individual sees life itself and what expectations they have of life experience.

When approached on the level of energy attunement, the Sun sign element represents a type of energy charge that needs to be fed or refueled often so that one's energy is not depleted. In other words, the element of your Sun sign is the fuel that you need

---

*See also Chapter 11 of *Astrology, Psychology & the Four Elements* for more on the meaning of the Sun sign's element. Chapter 14 of that same book also has considerable important material on all the planets' elemental placements.

to feel alive! It is the power which enables us to revitalize ourselves in order to cope with the stresses and demands of daily life.

SUN IN FIRE SIGNS:

Basically motivated by inspirations and aspirations

Recharges energy through vigorous, physically demanding activity and by pursuing new visions for the future

SUN IN EARTH SIGNS:

Basically motivated by material needs and practicality

Recharges energy through working with the physical world, being productive, feeding the senses

SUN IN AIR SIGNS:

Basically motivated by intellectual concepts and social ideals

Recharges energy through social involvement and intellectual stimulation

SUN IN WATER SIGNS:

Basically motivated by deep emotional yearnings and desires

Recharges energy through intense emotional experience and intimate involvement with people

The Moon

The element of the Moon's sign represents an attunement from the past that manifests automatically, a mode of feeling and being that one needs to be aware of in order to feel inwardly secure and at home with oneself. This element and experiences related to it feed your need to feel *right* about yourself; by such modes of self-expression, you are satisfying a deep inner need that can give stability to your entire personality. The Moon's element also shows how you react instinctively to all experiences, with what energy you spontaneously adjust yourself to the flow of life.

MOON IN FIRE SIGNS:

> Reacts to changing experiences with direct action and enthusiasm
>
> Feels comfortable when expressing confidence and strength

MOON IN EARTH SIGNS:

> Reacts to changing experiences with steadiness and stability
>
> Feels comfortable with self when being productive and working toward goals

MOON IN AIR SIGNS:

> Reacts to changing experiences with forethought and objective evaluation
>
> Feels comfortable with self when expressing ideas and interacting socially

MOON IN WATER SIGNS:

> Reacts to changing experiences with sensitivity and emotion
>
> Feels comfortable with self when feelings are deeply involved

Mercury

The element of Mercury's sign indicates what specific energy and quality influences one's thought processes, and how one expresses thoughts along that specific vibratory wavelength. Mercury symbolizes the urge to establish contact and true give-and-take communication with others, as well as all forms of coordination, including one's own nervous system coordination. Its element in a particular chart represents the inflow (through perception) and the outflow (through skill, speech, and manual dexterity) of intelligence. It shows the need to be understood by other people who are attuned to ideas in a similar way, as well as the need to learn by receiving ideas and information from the outer world.

MERCURY IN FIRE SIGNS:

Thoughts are influenced by one's aspirations, beliefs, hopes, and future visions

Skill and speech are expressed impulsively, demonstratively, and ethusiastically

MERCURY IN EARTH SIGNS:

Thoughts are influenced by practical considerations and colored by traditional attitudes

Skill and speech are expressed persistently, patiently, cautiously, and specifically

MERCURY IN WATER SIGNS:

Thoughts are influenced by one's deep feelings and yearnings

Skill and speech are expressed sensitively, emotionally, intuitively

MERCURY IN AIR SIGNS:

Thoughts are real things in themselves and are influenced by abstract ideals and by social considerations

Skill and speech are expressed objectively, articulately, and with understanding of the principles involved

Venus

Like Mercury, Venus represents an inflow and outflow of energy, and its placement in the various elements is expressed as the give and take of love, affection, and sensual pleasure with others. The element of one's Venus represents how one expresses affection and caring and how one gives of one's own feelings. That is the outflowing phase of the Venus principle in action, but the inflowing phase is equally important. It represents the sorts of experiences and types of expression that feed one's need for closeness with others and help one to feel loved and appreciated.

Venus in women has to do with the female ego. A woman needs to experience the qualities of her Venus sign in order to feel feminine. It also shows how a woman receives and gives of herself in love and sex. Venus is usually more of a sexual indicator for women than it is for men. It indicates how a woman approaches any relationship that might eventually lead to sex, as well as less intimate social relationships.

For a man, Venus is associated with romance, beauty, and with images that are especially lovely and attractive to him. It describes the type of woman that erotically attracts a man, that looks good to him aesthetically and turns on his feelings.* Venus is also related to a man's ideals about love, sex, and relationships. It is not usually specifically sexual, however; Mars is much more a symbol of sexual energy in men. In women, though, Venus and Mars energies are both important components of the sexual nature, and they combine and are usually more inseparable than is the case in most men.

VENUS IN FIRE SIGNS:

Affection and appreciation are expressed energetically, directly, and grandly

Feels love and closeness with another through sharing vigorous activities and mutual aspirations and enthusiasms

VENUS IN EARTH SIGNS:

Affection and appreciation are expressed tangibly, dependably, and physically

Feels love and closeness with another through commitment and building a life together, as well as through sensual pleasure and sharing responsibilities

---

*The emphasis in Venus is turning on the more erotically charged and sensual, romantic feelings. The Moon in a man's chart represents the type of woman that can attract a man on various other companionship levels and can turn on his feelings in other ways, such as needs for security, support, nurturing, and overall responsiveness.

VENUS IN AIR SIGNS:

Affection and appreciation are expressed through intense intellectual communication and a sense of companionship

Feels love and closeness with another through verbal sharing, a meeting of minds, mutually pleasant socializing

VENUS IN WATER SIGNS:

Affection and appreciation are expressed emotionally and sympathetically

Feels love and closeness with another through interchange of sensitivity and feelings on a subtle level, leading to a feeling of deep merging

Mars

The element of Mars shows what types of experiences and modes of activity stimulate one's physical energy and with what energy one seeks to assert oneself. The element of one's Mars is the energy that feeds your need for physical excitement and the mode through which you can express your aggressive powers to prove your strength. It describes the specific method you use to get what you want: *Mars in air* uses persuasion; *Mars in fire* uses power and initiative; *Mars in earth* uses patience and efficiency; and *Mars in water* uses intuition, slyness, and a rather unconquerable persistence.

For a man, Mars shows how he projects himself forcefully, assertively, and sexually. It indicates how he gives of his power in a sexual relationship, and how he expresses his masculinity in all areas of leadership and initiative. Thus, it is connected with a man's "male ego."

In a woman's chart, Mars is also a strong male image in her psyche; it is closely associated with a romantically exciting image that turns on her own energy and helps her to express herself.

The Mars sign and aspects often are a key to what kind of man a woman finds physically attractive.

MARS IN FIRE SIGNS:

Asserts self through direct physical action, initiative, and outgoing radiation of energy

Physical energy stimulated by constant movement, confident enthusiasm, and dynamic action

MARS IN EARTH SIGNS:

Asserts self through concrete achievement requiring patience and persistence

Physical energy stimulated by hard work, self-discipline, challenge, and duty

MARS IN AIR SIGNS:

Asserts self through expression of ideas, active communication, and energetic imagination

Physical energy stimulated by mental challenges, social activism, relationships, and new ideas

MARS IN WATER SIGNS:

Asserts self through emotional subtlety and persistence, and by appealing to the deeper feelings and needs of others

Physical energy stimulated by deep yearnings, feeling needed by others, subtle intuitions, and intensity of emotional experience

Jupiter

Jupiter's element shows what sorts of experiences and modes of activity generate an inner faith and confidence in oneself. To state this another way, one is able to experience a protective feeling of unity with a greater power or plan and a sense of well-being when one operates on the level indicated by Jupiter's element. Opportunities come through expression of that element's energy. It indicates a reservoir of vitality that is abundant and naturally flowing, thus contributing to one's health.

JUPITER IN FIRE SIGNS:

Inner faith comes when one is outgoing, enthusiastic, assertive, and physically active

Opportunities are stimulated when one takes risks to express oneself and try new things

JUPITER IN EARTH SIGNS:

Inner faith comes when one tunes into practicality, dependability, and the experiences of the senses

Opportunities are stimulated when one works hard, assumes responsibilities, and tunes in to nature and its rhythm

JUPITER IN AIR SIGNS:

Inner faith is stimulated through exploring new ideas, communicating with new people, and social improvement

Opportunities come when one expresses ideas enthusiastically and interacts with others for a future goal

JUPITER IN WATER SIGNS:

Inner faith is stimulated through depth of emotional experience and through positive expression of one's compassion and imagination

Opportunities come when one is sensitive and caring toward others, and when one intuitively follows one's inner yearnings

Saturn

The element of Saturn in one's chart generally indicates a challenge; one is working toward fully accepting, without fear, the level of experience represented by that particular element. This fear is often an outgrowth of an old pattern of life that has now become intolerably rigid and oppressive; the caution and discipline connected with this pattern may still be useful for one's growth, *if* it is accepted as a motivating force toward consistent, concrete expression in that area of life.

Saturn's element indicates at what level of expression one tends to be inhibited and where one's energy is blocked or restricted. This inner blockage arises because that level of experience is overly-important to the individual. He or she therefore tends to be tied up in knots in this area of life. By trying too hard to express the energy, or by avoiding or repressing it, one tends to restrict the natural flow of the energy.

SATURN IN FIRE SIGNS:

> Need to stabilize one's identity and express creative energy with more regularity and objectivity

> Effort should be put into freer self-expression with both enthusiasm and responsibility

SATURN IN EARTH SIGNS:

> Need to stabilize one's efficiency and precision in work and in handling daily responsibilities

> Effort should be put into mastering the physical world and developing a systematic approach

SATURN IN AIR SIGNS:

> Need to stabilize one's thinking and discipline one's mind without lapsing into negative thinking

> Effort should be put into communicating clearly and practically, as well as effectively handling social responsibilities with sincerity while still maintaining a detached perspective

SATURN IN WATER SIGNS:

> Need to stabilize one's emotions and sensitivities, expressing feelings while simultaneously developing more detachment from them

Effort should be put into expressing feelings with self-acceptance while disciplining over-sensitivity

Uranus, Neptune & Pluto in the Elements

For understanding the birth chart of an individual, the element placements of these three outer planets are relatively unimportant. Each of these three planets remains in a certain element (and sign) for quite a few years, and thus little *individualized* meaning can be derived from such a widespread factor. The elemental emphasis revealed by the outer planets' placements over a period of some years is primarily of interest for illuminating generational differences and subtler changes in mass psychology worldwide.

CHAPTER 5

THE PLANETS IN THE SIGNS

Zodiacal Signs & Their Key Concepts

	KEY CONCEPT	A planet in this sign will be colored by these qualities
FIRE SIGNS		
CARDINAL: ARIES	Single-pointed release of energy toward *new* experience	Self-willed urge for action, self-assertion
FIXED: LEO	Sustained warmth of loyalty and radiant vitalization	Pride and urge for recognition, sense of drama
MUTABLE: SAGITTARIUS	Restless aspiration propelling one toward an ideal	Beliefs, generalizations, ideals
EARTH SIGNS		
CARDINAL: CAPRICORN	Impersonal determination to get things done	Self-control, caution, reserve and ambition
FIXED: TAURUS	Depth of appreciation related to immediate physical sensations	Possessiveness, retentiveness, steadiness
MUTABLE: VIRGO	Spontaneous helpfulness, humility, & need to serve	Perfectionism, analysis, fine discrimination

	KEY CONCEPT	*A planet in this sign will be colored by these qualities*
AIR SIGNS		
CARDINAL: **LIBRA**	Harmonization of all polarities for self-completion	Balance, impartiality, tact
FIXED: **AQUARIUS**	Detached coordination of all people and concepts	Individualistic freedom, extremism
MUTABLE: **GEMINI**	Immediate perception and verbalization of all connections	Changeable curiosity, talkativeness, friendliness
WATER SIGNS		
CARDINAL: **CANCER**	Instinctive nurturing and protective empathy	Feeling, reserve, moods, sensitivity, self-protection
FIXED: **SCORPIO**	Penetration through intense emotional power	Compulsive desires, depth, controlled passion, secrecy
MUTABLE: **PISCES**	Healing compassion for all that suffers	Soul-yearnings, idealism, oneness, inspiration, vulnerability

Functions of the Planets in the Signs

The sign position of this planet shows:

These five are commonly called the "personal planets."

SUN:	how one is (the tone of being) and how one experiences life & expresses one's individuality
MOON:	how one reacts based on subconscious predisposition
MERCURY:	how one thinks & communicates
VENUS:	how one expresses *affection, feels appreciated, & gives of self*
MARS:	how one asserts *self & expresses desires*

These two planets are a complementary pair and serve as a bridge between small personal concerns and larger concerns of principle and society.

JUPITER:	how one seeks to *grow, improve oneself, & experience trust in life*
SATURN:	how one seeks to *establish & preserve self through effort*

These three outer planets represent profound sources of change and can be referred to as "transformative" planets or energies.

The sign positions of URANUS, NEPTUNE, and PLUTO are indications of generational attitudes, but in the individual chart their signs are of much less importance than their house positions and aspects.

The Sun in the Signs—
Interpretive Guidelines

THE SIGN POSITION OF THE SUN: How one is (the individual's tone of being) and how one experiences life & expresses one's individuality

Interpretive Guidelines for Sun in Aries:

Radiates forceful, confident vitality

Tries to fill need for recognition with self-assertion and direct, competitive actions

Forceful assertion of individuality is necessary for full self-expression

Identifies self as explorer, pioneer, the first to begin an adventure; quickly grasps essentials

May antagonize others with too-forceful expression of individuality

Interpretive Guidelines for Sun in Taurus:

Vitality is rooted in earthy physical sensations

Needs to be recognized for reliability, ability to produce

Creative expression results in tangible objects or in gathered resources

Takes pride in possessions, assets, and in one's own stability

Expression of individuality can be hindered by hesitation and reluctance to change

Interpretive Guidelines for Sun in Gemini:

Creative energy directed toward perception, acquiring facts, asking questions, and toward finding connections between ideas

Needs to express self verbally, and to receive recognition for intellectual abilities

Radiates changeable, talkative, mental energy

Free connection of ideas and a wide variety of social contacts are necessary for full self-expression

Sustained effort in one area is difficult to maintain due to a wide variety of interests

Interpretive Guidelines for Sun in Cancer:

Experiences strength through nurturing, sensitive, mother-like qualities

Feels instinctive urge to protect one's ego; builds inner self a nest from which it can safely radiate

Levels of vitality and creative energy depend on moods, and so are difficult to maintain

Expresses self creatively through emotions, and feels need to be recognized for sensitivity

Sense of individuality is expressed most clearly in a familiar, sheltered environment or situation

Interpretive Guidelines for Sun in Leo:

Expresses self with warmly radiant vitality and constant need to be noticed

Creative energy is colored by a sense of drama and bigness

Motivated by a need to be recognized for one's generosity

Radiates confidence and encouragement to others; can vitalize any enterprise

Pride is a dominant personality characteristic; heartfelt, but childlike, emotions are always at work

Interpretive Guidelines for Sun in Virgo:

Directs creative energy analytically and with discrimination

Motivated by a need to be helpful, to be of service in a tangible way

Radiates intelligence and clean-edged vitality

Attunement of soul to essential values, service, and constant need to improve oneself

Humble, unassuming sense of individuality can interfere with public recognition

Interpretive Guidelines for Sun in Libra:

☉ Creative energy directed toward interpersonal relationships and initiating ideas

♎ Needs to be recognized for impartiality, fairness, kindness, and ability to harmonize opposing energies

Radiates sociable, graceful, intellectual vitality and a refined sensitivity to beauty

Constant urge to create balance in one's relationships and lifestyle

Sense of individuality can be obliterated through over-concentration on pleasing others

Interpretive Guidelines for Sun in Scorpio:

☉ Creative energy penetrates surface experience through intense emotional power and intuition

♏ Needs to express one's transformative energy, often into re-forming the status quo

Craving for intensity, involving the core of human experience, often seeking this in deep, merging (usually highly sexual) relationships

Level of vitality is connected to constant inner compulsive desires—sometimes obsessions

Flow of creative expression can be hindered by emotional fixations, reluctance to be open, and fear of losing control

Interpretive Guidelines for Sun in Sagittarius:

☉ Creative energy is directed toward one's ideals and apsirations, not only expressing them but often promoting them ♐ to others

Sense of individuality is colored by one's ultimate beliefs and optimistic philosophical outlook

Essentially values wide-ranging mental and physical liberty

Radiates a friendly, exploratory, open spirit—very broad-minded and values honesty

Needs to be recognized for moral, upright nature; sometimes high standards can lead to intolerance and insensitivity to others

Interpretive Guidelines for Sun in Capricorn:

Creative energy colored by self-control, caution, traditionalism

Essentially values hard work, authority, and achievement

Needs to work single-mindedly and with discipline toward well-defined goals in order to fully express self

Level of vitality is affected and sense of individuality is developed by one's ability to assume responsibility

Flow of creative expression can be frozen by pessimism, a cynical attitude, or too much concern with respectability and appearances

Interpretive Guidelines for Sun in Aquarius:

Creative energy is directed toward society's welfare and theoretical concepts, especially through innovation

Radiates friendly, people-oriented mental energy—often with a tinge of extremism

Urge to be and to create is colored by freedom, eccentricity, and experimentation

Essentially values humanity and the world of the intellect, with the need to find what's "right" or "true"

Expression of individuality can be deterred by self-effacement, over-concentration on duty, or aimless rebellion

Interpretive Guidelines for Sun in Pisces:

Creative energy is expressed sensitively and inspirationally

Needs to be recognized for compassionate, giving nature

Sense of individuality is not clearly focused, due to empathy with lives and problems of others

Radiates a healing and compassionate spirit toward all that suffers

Vitality and self-expression are colored by soul-yearnings, overwhelming vulnerability, and the state of the inner life

The Moon in the Signs—
Interpretive Guidelines

THE SIGN POSITION OF THE MOON: How one reacts based on subconscious predisposition

Interpretive Guidelines for Moon in Aries:

☽ Reacts aggressively, impatiently, forcefully, directly, competitively

♈ A need for self-assertion in order to feel emotionally secure and right about oneself

A confident, action-oriented sense of self focused on *new* experience

Responds to experience and environment with a single-pointed release of energy

Combative qualities can hinder attainment of security

Interpretive Guidelines for Moon in Taurus:

☽ Reacts slowly to any experience; maintains stability and poise when faced with outer demands

♉ Inner contentment comes through waiting, stillness, relating to the world of nature

Flows into physical sensations, emotionally retaining the feeling of touching and savoring the pleasures of the moment

Inner self slow to change; retains habit patterns for a long time, which can result in stubbornness or laziness

Feels secure in unchanging, predictable situations and comfortable with all sensual stimuli

Emphasis on possessiveness and a deep need for security and control can inhibit emotional flow

Interpretive Guidelines for Moon in Gemini:

☽ Reacts quickly, perceptively, changeably, with unending curiosity

♊ Feels secure in responding to a variety of mental stimuli, and in being involved in more than one activity at a time

Adapts to change by using the mind and making connections

Communicates about inner emotional life; a need to verbalize emotions in order to feel connected with them

Sense of security can be deterred by emotional energy scattered in many directions

Interpretive Guidelines for Moon in Cancer:

☽ Reacts with sensitivity (sometimes over-sensitivity) and with protectiveness (toward self and others)

♋ Feels secure when nurturing and being nurtured by others

Natural sense of timing and ability to tune in to intuitions and emotional subtleties

Extremely sensitive to moods and reactions of others; often at the mercy of one's own moods

Can be over-protective of emotions; strong memory of past emotions is retained forever, still coloring attitudes toward present situations

Interpretive Guidelines for Moon in Leo:

☽ Reacts warmly, generously, enthusiastically

♌ Feeling of emotional security comes from pride and confidence in self

Puts much creative energy into the environment and can be supportive and encouraging toward others

Adapts to life by dramatizing, creating new situations, using humor to entertain others

Confident, creative, self-image underlies all actions—often a childlike simplicity

Constant radiation of proud, outgoing feelings can interfere with ones receptivity

Interpretive Guidelines for Moon in Virgo:

Reacts with practical adaptation to all stimuli

Responds analytically to all experiences; needs a sense of order in the environment to feel comfortable

Refines emotional reactions in order to perfect their expression

Serving others and being helpful contribute to positive self-image and help overcome innate tendency toward guilt and self-doubt

Feels secure through analysis of the physical and emotional world, and through making definite, concrete improvements

Need to dissect emotions can inhibit responsiveness

Interpretive Guidelines for Moon in Libra:

Reacts with objectivity to the environment and all experiences, with a strongly developed sense of fairness

Thinks before reacting; weighs all sides of a situation, which can contribute to indecisiveness

Finding balance and harmonization of polarities is necessary for emotional tranquility; eager to please and to see the other's point of view

Feels secure when involved in close relationships; uncomfortable being alone for long

Emphasis on gracious demeanor can inhibit spontaneity of emotional reactions and real intimacy

Interpretive Guidelines for Moon in Scorpio:

☽ Reacts intensely, passionately, with controlled emotional power

♏ Self-image affected by complex, turbulent emotions; confidence sometimes undermined by negative emotions or supported by passionate sense of purpose

Depth of feelings and secretiveness contribute to person's mystique and charisma

A need to deeply penetrate experiences leads to comprehension of underlying motives or to imagining all sorts of fearful motives in others

Feels nurtured when giving and/or receiving intense emotional energy

Fear of vulnerability and losing control can lead to emotional repression

Interpretive Guidelines for Moon in Sagittarius:

☽ Reacts enthusiastically and idealistically, based on beliefs and philosophy

♐ Inner contentment felt when aspiring toward or promoting one's ideals, or when progressing toward one's future goals

Subconscious predisposition to question, to search for meaning—an innate broad-minded, tolerant, buoyant attitude toward life

Feels comfortable when exploring, travelling, being outdoors; loves a sense of freedom

Orientation toward emotional beliefs can lead to gullibility, arrogance, fanaticism, or a pretentious preachiness

Interpretive Guidelines for Moon in Capricorn:

☽ Reacts with self-control and determination; sometimes reacts automatically with severe negativity

♑ Needs to manipulate the world and others in order to feel secure, comfortable, and to achieve one's goals; can set aside personal concerns to fulfill duties

Controlled response to experience; cautiously projects authoritative, determined energy

Feels comfortable in role of provider, protector; habitually takes control of situations

Dominant emotional need to be on top or to be an authority can limit capacity for intimacy and emotional nurturing

Interpretive Guidelines for Moon in Aquarius:

Reacts unpredictably, eccentrically, and with detached objectivity

Feels secure when exercising complete freedom of ideas, self-expression, and innovation

Responds individualistically, based on sense of self as unique, altruistic, and socially conscious

Needs to interact socially in order to feel emotionally centered and right about self

Nurtures others by encouraging their freedom, and feels supported when given complete autonomy in return

A need for emotional independence can cause alienation from one's true feelings and aloofness toward the sensitivities of others

Interpretive Guidelines for Moon in Pisces:

Reacts sensitively, compassionately, empathetically, evasively, vulnerably, idealistically

Periods of unfocused, freely imaginative daydreaming help bring emotional tranquility

Needs a sense of oneness with the world and the universe to feel secure and right about oneself

Nurtures others through healing compassion and sympathy; feels secure when serving humanity or a spiritual ideal

Feelings about self are nebulous, which can inhibit self-understanding and confidence

Flows easily with changing situations; contentment comes through giving of self and/or transcending the personal self and its fears

Mercury in the Signs— Interpretive Guidelines

THE SIGN POSITION OF MERCURY: How One Thinks & Communicates

Interpretive Guidelines for Mercury in Aries:

Communicates assertively, forcefully, directly, confidently

Restless urge for action underlies energetic way of speaking and creative use of skills

Confrontation and forceful release of energy are necessary in order to learn; capacity to intuitively grasp essentials

Reasoning ability is colored by a self-willed release of energy toward new experience; daring new thoughts are therefore often preferred

Establishing true give-and-take with others can be hindered by insensitive and inconsiderate self-assertion

Interpretive Guidelines for Mercury in Taurus:

Communicates carefully, making sure of each word before saying it; slow expression of one's thoughts

A need to learn slowly and deliberately can limit the variety of one's perceptions

A retentive, steady mind, based on consolidation of ideas; brings ideas down to earth for practical application

Urge to express one's perceptions of physical sensations; tangibly savoring one's words while speaking

The need to establish connections with others is restricted by a reluctance to share self freely and spontaneously

Interpretive Guidelines for Mercury in Gemini:

Communicates fluently, quickly, cleverly, and intelligently— sometimes superficially

Urge to express perceptions immediately

Needs to learn through establishing and identifying connections among people and ideas

Changeably curious mind expresses itself through friendly interactions with others and through endless questions

High level of nervous energy is expressed through talking, writing, or other forms of manual/mental dexterity

Interpretive Guidelines for Mercury in Cancer:

Communicates emotionally, instinctively, and sensitively; is protective of one's own thoughts

Learns through absorption, relying on feelings to make connections between bits of information

Nurtures new ideas until they blossom as creative skill

Good memory and retentive qualities contribute to learning abilities

Subconscious prejudices and fears can interfere with objectivity and attention to new ideas

Interpretive Guidelines for Mercury in Leo:

Communicates energetically, radiantly, and proudly

Warmth, affection, and strong will motivate the need to establish connections

Communication colored by sense of drama, humor, and creative flair

Pride and urge for recognition spark expression of perceptions

Needs creative involvement in order to learn; makes intuitive leaps rather than logical associations

Ego's involvement with thinking process can obliterate objectivity and limit flexibility and retention of facts

Interpretive Guidelines for Mercury in Virgo:

☿ ♍ Communicates logically, critically, helpfully, humbly—sometimes negatively and skeptically

An urge to express one's perceptions matter-of-factly, demonstrating one's analytical skills

A need to discriminate among ideas and to put them in logical sequence in order to learn

Practical, helpful ideas contribute to the ability to make connections with others

Over-attention to details can hinder perception of the larger viewpoint and all its interconnections and broader implications

Interpretive Guidelines for Mercury in Libra:

☿ ♎ Communicates intelligently, personably, diplomatically, and elegantly

Urge to express one's perceptions harmoniously—in a fair-minded, objective mode—to balance all polarities

Needs to be impartial and tactful in order to establish connections with others

Verbal expression is colored by an artistic, aesthetic sense

Seeks balance and objectivity in personal interactions, and needs feedback on ideas to clarify them

Awareness of all points of view can hinder the ability to come to a decision

Interpretive Guidelines for Mercury in Scorpio:

☿ ♏ Communicates powerfully, deeply, and passionately (often non-verbally!); can form deeply intimate bonds through communication

Urge for verbal expression comes from the depths of one's being and is never superficial

A profound need to learn by penetrating and probing to the core of reality; very thorough in all research and interested in detection

Objective understanding can be hindered by the overly-intense, willful, and emotional nature of the mind

Use of skill and intelligence are influenced by powerful desires, deep passions, and the urge to discover others' hidden motivations

Ability to establish connections with others can be inhibited by the need for secrecy and silence

Interpretive Guidelines for Mercury in Sagittarius:

 Communicates openly, truthfully, optimistically, enthusiastically, and tolerantly

 The need to learn is expressed through restless aspiration propelling one toward an ideal

Thinking and reasoning are guided by long-term goals rather than mundane details

Interest in teaching others what one has learned; learning and teaching are seen as closely related

Need to establish connections with others by being direct, truthful, and broad-minded

Coherent thinking can be blurred by the over-generalizations that idealistic aspirations motivate

Interpretive Guidelines for Mercury in Capricorn:

 Communicates seriously, cautiously, with a strong sense of authority; sometimes thinks in rigid categories

 Persistence, ambition, and steady progress satisfy one's need to learn

Self-controlled urge to express one's perceptions and intelligence through manipulation of the physical world, and to get practical results from theories

Reserved, self-sufficient, formal qualities can inhibit the way one communicates with others

Reason and power of discrimination are used to build toward a goal; keen awareness of practical reality can lead to a focus on limitations rather than possibilities

Interpretive Guidelines for Mercury in Aquarius:

 Communicates openly, intelligently, idealistically, in a detached manner

 Needs to establish unique connections with others, relating individualistically with each person, while having strong awareness of group communication processes

Urge to express one's perceptions and intelligence is colored by individualistic freedom and often by extremism

Thinks experimentally and innovatively, testing theories on others; future-oriented, likes to explore possibilities for change

Independent, inventive, detached intellectual qualities contribute to the learning process

Expression of ideas can be erratic—fragmented by unpredictable connections between unrelated concepts

Interpretive Guidelines for Mercury in Pisces:

 Communicates sensitively, idealistically, poetically, evasively, imaginatively

Compassion motivates one to express perceptions and intelligence sympathetically

Establishes connections with others psychically and spiritually; communication is perceived on more than one level

Verbal energy is inspired by flexibility and the power of synthesis

Reason and power of discrimination can be clouded by confusion, daydreaming, and self-deception

Venus in the Signs— Interpretive Guidelines

THE SIGN POSITION OF VENUS: How one expresses affection, feels appreciated, & gives of self

Interpretive Guidelines for Venus in Aries:

♀
♈

Expresses affection directly, impulsively, enthusiastically

Emotionally-colored tastes and pleasures blossom when energy is directed toward new experience; especially enjoys the first stages of relationships

Need to feel close to another can be thwarted by strong self-assertive, demanding qualities; intimacy therefore sometimes difficult to achieve

Values individuality, initiative, and independence in self and others

Gives of self energetically, and responds to forceful release of energy from others

Interpretive Guidelines for Venus in Taurus:

♀
♉

Expresses affection physically, warmly, steadily, possessively

Gives from self's inner resources; responds to sensual, deeply-centered energy from others

A need to give of one's affections can be hampered by emotional stinginess, possessiveness, or reluctance to release feelings or lose control

Deeply appreciates physical sensations: sight, sound, smell, taste, and touch; enjoys contact with nature

Values material comfort, luxury, and beautiful physical objects

Interpretive Guidelines for Venus in Gemini:

♀ Expresses affection verbally, cleverly, lightly, playfully

♊ Needs to talk immediately about one's thoughts and perceptions in order to feel close to another

Emotionally-colored tastes are constantly and consciously changing; variety and mental rapport are highly valued

Urge for pleasure is colored by changeable curiosity, talkativeness, and friendliness; attracted to intelligence and quick wit

Need for variety and constant new stimuli can inhibit chances for lasting relationships and interpersonal depth beyond the superficial

Interpretive Guidelines for Venus in Cancer:

♀ Expresses affection sensitively, comfortingly, protectively, tenaciously

♋ Need to nurture and be nurtured, to feel part of a family, in order to be comfortable

Prefers to share energy with others within an enclosed, close-knit group

Urge for pleasure and closeness can be hampered by moodiness, timidity, stinginess, or overly self-protective feelings; easily reflects others' pleasures and moods

Receptive and dependent qualities are always involved in feeling close to another

Interpretive Guidelines for Venus in Leo:

♀ Expresses affection warmly, dramatically, enthusiastically

♌ Emotionally-colored tastes are influenced by one's pride and an urge for recognition

Gives of self with creative vitality, and receives from others graciously and proudly

Sociability and expressions of love are colored by playfulness, generosity, and loyalty

Exchange of deeper feelings with another may be encumbered by one's need to be the center of attention or to dominate the other's emotional life

Interpretive Guidelines for Venus in Virgo:

Expresses affection matter-of-factly, modestly, helpfully, timidly

A need to serve and be useful yields emotional satisfaction

Finds pleasure in precise attention to details and analytical mental activity

A need for logic and practicality in order to feel comfortable and harmonious

Over-helpfulness, petty criticisms, or one's natural reserve can interfere with emotional give-and-take and the expression of passion

Interpretive Guidelines for Venus in Libra:

Expresses affection lightly, considerately, charmingly, and harmoniously

Give-and-take with others is colored by balance, fairness, and gentleness

Emotionally-colored tastes are affected by a need to harmonize polarities and to appreciate symmetry and traditional beauty

A deep need for peace, tranquility, and harmony in order to feel comfort and pleasure, but this could lead to avoidance of unpleasant emotional interchanges and thus limit the scope of intimacy

Needs to develop relationships based on equal sharing and cooperation in order to give of one's emotions

Interpretive Guidelines for Venus in Scorpio:

♀ Expresses affection intensely, passionately, obsessively, with extreme, consuming feelings

♏ Urge for pleasure is colored by compulsive desires, depth, and passionate emotions

Give-and-take with others generates a healing, transformative energy

Social and love needs can be hindered by inclination to secrecy and reluctance to trust others

Needs to penetrate deeply into a relationship with intense emotional power in order to feel close to another

Interpretive Guidelines for Venus in Sagittarius:

♀ Expresses affection freely, enthusiastically, generously, and idealistically

♐ Restless urge to move onward and have many adventures can interfere with establishing close relationships

How one relates to others is highly colored by one's beliefs and goals, and a philosophical harmony is needed in close relationships

A need for freedom to roam and explore in order to feel comfort and harmony

Attitudes toward love and romance are tolerant and broadminded; values honesty in relationships and may insensitively overlook others' feelings

Interpretive Guidelines for Venus in Capricorn:

♀ Expresses affection cautiously, seriously, dutifully, and mechanically

♑ Pleasure and love needs can be inhibited by fearful, suspicious attitudes or an aloof, impersonal approach

Needs to be sure of commitment from another before giving of self's deeper emotions; capable of loyalty and of facing the work and responsibilities of relationships

Social and love urge is colored by perserverance, ambition, conservatism, and concern for reputation

Need for self-control and emotional reserve can hamper the development of close relationships

Interpretive Guidelines for Venus in Aquarius:

♀ Expresses affection freely, unconventionally, flirtatiously, experimentally

♒ Detached, impersonal attitude can interfere with close relationships; others may consider the person cold and aloof

Enjoys exchange of theories, ideas, and imaginative (often humorous) fantasies with a loved one

Love and social urges are colored by individualistic freedom, extremism, and rebelliousness

Need for active socializing with many people in order to give fully of self's emotions

Interpretive Guidelines for Venus in Pisces:

♀ Expresses affection sensitively, kindly, compassionately, and sympathetically; capable of selfless giving

♓ A need for a magical and romantic harmony is deeply felt; but desires can be unfocused and vague, leaving the person vulnerable

Social and love urge colored by romantic idealism; one idealizes loved ones and love itself

Escapism, evasion, and confusion can undermine the ability to give of self and to receive from others, and lack of discrimination can hamper forming solid relationships

Feelings of closeness with another are influenced by soul-yearnings and an urge to mingle psychically with the other person; empathy arises from ability to identify with others' feelings

Mars in the Signs— Interpretive Guidelines

THE SIGN POSITION OF MARS: How one asserts self & expresses desires

Interpretive Guidelines for Mars in Aries:

♂
♈ Asserts self competitively, directly, impatiently

Single-pointed release of physical energy directed toward new experience; often a flair for starting new businesses and/or mechanical ingenuity

Self-willed urge for action is strongly directed toward one's desires; faces obstacles directly, but recklessness can impede success

Initiative, willpower, and restlessness characterize the method of operation, as well as an intuitive grasp of essentials

Sexual drive and physical energy are expressed impulsively, powerfully, and confidently

Interpretive Guidelines for Mars in Taurus:

♂
♉ Asserts self steadily, retentively, conservatively, stubbornly

Strong actions are directed toward consolidation, productivity, and enjoyment of simple pleasures; often a creative and/or artistic flair

Initiative and drive are colored by material concerns and possessiveness, and sometimes by slowness and laziness

Achievement of desires may be thwarted by complacency and satisfaction with things as they are

Physical energy and sexual drive are influenced by deep appreciation of the physical senses and natural rhythms of life

Interpretive Guidelines for Mars in Gemini:

♂ Asserts self flexibly, verbally, cleverly, communicatively, through a wide variety of specialized skills

♊ The focus of one's desires changes quickly and often; frequently uncertain of what one wants and thus easily diverted

Physical energy and sexual drive are affected by mentally-stimulating conversations, images, or curious new ideas—very open-minded

Decisiveness is influenced by momentary situations and immediate perceptions

Action and initiative are directed toward making connections, using one's mind to learn new facts and develop new skills, and expressing a wide-ranging friendliness

Interpretive Guidelines for Mars in Cancer:

♂ Asserts self sensitively, shyly, indirectly, and sympathetically

♋ A need to feel connected with one's roots and traditions in order to clarify one's desires and understand one's direction in life

Initiative and willpower can be hindered by moodiness and cautious self-protection, but capable of fearless action to support loved ones

Physical and sexual energy and decisiveness are inhibited by unconscious feelings, fears, and vulnerabilities, and stimulated by feeling cared for and protected

One pursues one's desires tenaciously and intuitively, with an instinct for self-preservation and a sense of timing in pursuit of goals

Interpretive Guidelines for Mars in Leo:

♂ Asserts self dramatically, warmly, radiantly, expressively, arrogantly

♌ Expressing desires is strongly colored by pride and an urge for recognition

Initiative and drive are expressed confidently, with creative flair and abundant vitality

Needs to be complimented and appreciated for sexual, physical, or creative prowess; physical and sexual energy is stimulated by attention and demonstrative generosity

Needs to express oneself assertively and dynamically in order to achieve one's desires; often becomes pushy and too dominating toward others

Interpretive Guidelines for Mars in Virgo:

♂ Asserts self modestly, helpfully, analytically, dutifully—sometimes with petty criticism

♍ Decisiveness, initiative, and method of operation are colored by perfectionism and fine discrimination

Strong actions can be hindered by self-criticism and over-attentiveness to details

An underlying need to serve influences the physical energy and the willpower; ability to work hard and vigorously with practical intelligence

Need to strive toward perfection in order to achieve desires

Interpretive Guidelines for Mars in Libra:

♂ Asserts self sociably, cooperatively, charmingly, with direct relatedness

♎ Desire to harmonize all polarities underlies one's will toward action

Physical energy and decisiveness are strongly affected by one's close relationships and by aesthetic influences

Initiative and drive are tactfully and tactically directed toward balance and fairness

Pursuit of one's desires can be hindered by indecisiveness while one weighs the options

Interpretive Guidelines for Mars in Scorpio:

Asserts self intensely, magnetically, passionately, and powerfully

Physical energy and initiative are prompted by strong desires, compulsions, and challenges; capable of great endurance

Sex urge is motivated by need to share deep emotional closeness and to experience profound intensity

Need to channel and transform emotional power in order to achieve desires effectively

Decisiveness and freedom of expression are hindered by secretiveness and the need for self-protection and total control

Interpretive Guidelines for Mars in Sagittarius:

Asserts self honestly, idealistically, energetically, impulsively, tactlessly

What one wants is guided by one's beliefs, morality, and inspirations

Decisiveness and strong actions are motivated by one's aspiration toward an ideal or a guiding vision of the future

Physical and sexual excitement is stimulated by adventurous activities

Initiative and drive are colored by an expansive urge for self-improvement and a restless need for exploration

Interpretive Guidelines for Mars in Capricorn:

Asserts self cautiously, seriously, authoritatively, ambitiously, with strong self-discipline

Decisiveness is accompanied by careful planning, calculation, and patience

Physical energy and drive are often directed toward personal material goals and long-term achievement

Pursues one's desires steadily and persistently through conventional channels

Sex urge is self-controlled, but strong and earthy

Interpretive Guidelines for Mars in Aquarius:

♂ Asserts self intelligently, individualistically, eccentrically, and independently

♒ Initiative and willpower are colored by a need for broad freedom of expression

Achievement of goals can be thwarted by rebelliousness, but reforming, revolutionizing urge can be channeled into creative innovations

Detachment and scientific objectivity can hinder the expression of passionate desires

Physical energy and sex drive are stimulated by a sense of freedom, experimentation, and the excitement of new possibilities and new ideas

Interpretive Guidelines for Mars in Pisces:

♂ Asserts self idealistically, empathetically, agreeably, with underlying kindness

♓ Initiative and will-power are colored by sensitivity and compassion for others

Self-assertion and decisiveness are encumbered by substantial personal and emotional vulnerability

Physical energy and sexual drive are always affected by dreams, moods, and emotions

One pursues one's desires subtly, motivated chiefly by inspiration, intuition, or a guiding vision

Jupiter in the Signs—
Interpretive Guidelines

THE SIGN POSITION OF JUPITER: How one seeks to grow, improve oneself, & experience trust in life

Interpretive Guidelines for Jupiter in Aries:

♃ ♈ Seeks to grow and improve oneself through confident, self-assertive activity

Needs to rely on one's own enterprise and energy in order to have faith in life—often well-developed leadership abilities

Opportunities arise through a single-pointed release of energy toward new experience

Too much aggression, force, and restlessness can lead to over-expansion, taking excessive risks, and missing opportunities for personal development

Has an innate understanding of the importance of courage and faith in oneself

Interpretive Guidelines for Jupiter in Taurus:

Seeks to grow and improve oneself through productivity, steadiness, and reliability

---

NOTE: The importance of Jupiter in the birth chart is underestimated in interpretation and in tradition. It actually guides us into the future and motivates future growth and development, especially along idealistic lines. Jupiter's deeper meanings are neglected, for the most part, and this is why these guidelines are sometimes more elaborate and detailed than those for other planets. In some ways, Jupiter is too simple a principle for a complex age, and it is too philosophical for a relativistic, materialistic age.

The Jupiter sign of any person is always a powerful personality tone. That sign's qualities often pervade the individual's personality and character. In many cases, the person has that sign's energy, abilities, and qualities in quite a highly developed state, although they will often be taken for granted by the person since that comes so easily and naturally. In short, not in all cases but in the majority of people, Jupiter elevates and enobles and thus expresses the more generous and positive side of its sign.

♃
♉ Urge to connect self with a larger order is fulfilled through deep appreciation of the physical world; has a highly-developed sensuality

Attempting to improve life solely through money, possessions, and luxury can lead to an overly-materialistic attitude and wastefulness

Has a broad and tolerant understanding of human nature and basic human needs for pleasure

Trust in life is enhanced by communication with nature and a simple existence; expresses the more noble and generous qualities of Taurus

Interpretive Guidelines for Jupiter in Gemini:

♃
♊ Seeks to grow and improve oneself through communication, developing a wide range of skills, and broad learning

Faith comes through immediate perception and verbalization of all connections; wide-ranging interests contribute meaning to life

Optimism is sometimes hindered by changeable curiosity and excessive thinking and worrying

Need to develop intelligence and reasoning power in order to experience trust in oneself and in life; an urge to connect with a larger order that is rational and logical

Has an innate understanding of the importance of good communication and a desire to benefit others by being a source of information

Interpretive Guidelines for Jupiter in Cancer:

♃
♋ Seeks to grow and improve oneself through development of family values and emotional supportiveness

Opportunities come through one's expression of protective empathy and instinctive nurturing

Need for sensitivity to others' feelings in order to have confidence in self; this emotional sensitivity is usually well-developed

Reliance on a higher power can be dampened by excessive reserve, fears, or self-protection

Has an innate understanding of the human need for security, and usually expresses the more giving, generous side of Cancer

Interpretive Guidelines for Jupiter in Leo:

Seeks to grow and improve oneself through creative activity, freely expressing one's exuberant vitality, and through warm, supportive encouragement of others

Expansiveness is colored by pride and an urge for recognition; intuitively understands people's needs for attention and self-confidence

Trust in a higher order can be hindered by egotism and an arrogant, domineering attitude, but usually has an innate and irrepressible faith in life

Need to act impressively and be recognized by others leads to confidence in self; has a well-developed sense of showmanship and flair

Expresses faith in life as a drama; feels blessed to be playing one's role in life, but sometimes has excessive faith in the importance of one's own role

Interpretive Guidelines for Jupiter in Virgo:

Seeks to grow and improve oneself through spontaneous helpfulness, dutiful service, and a disciplined approach to self-development

Humbly stays open to grace from a higher power, and naturally trusts the value of regular work and self-discipline

Expansive need for perfection motivates openness to self-improvement

Over-attention to detail can inhibit connection with a larger order, but usually has a well-developed critical faculty without excessive pettiness

Has an innate understanding of the appropriate use of one's analytical and discriminative abilities

Interpretive Guidelines for Jupiter in Libra:

♃
♎ Seeks to grow and improve oneself through a balanced and objective attitude, fair-mindedness, and a diplomatic approach

One's faith is enhanced through a balanced, impartial, broad-minded attitude

Opportunities arise through one's close relationships, and the capacity for sincere one-to-one interchange is usually well-developed

Urge toward a larger order is expressed through sharing, cooperation, and encouraging others—sometimes through art or beauty

A need to weigh all sides of a question may undermine confident expansive actions and decisive thinking

Interpretive Guidelines for Jupiter in Scorpio:

♃
♏ Seeks to grow and improve oneself through transmutation of desires and compulsions and by unusually thorough understanding of life's inner workings

Opportunities come through one's ability to shrewdly judge people and situations—a well-developed sense of resourcefulness and opportunism

Optimistic expansion and developing faith can be hindered by fear, secrecy, and the inability to open up emotionally; but Jupiter often expresses the nobler and more elevated qualities of Scorpio

Urge to connect with something greater than self is expressed through intensity of experience and depth of feeling;

trust in a higher power comes through seeking and confronting that intensity

Need to tap into a powerful transformative energy in order to have confidence in self

Interpretive Guidelines for Jupiter in Sagittarius:

Seeks to grow and improve oneself through aspiration toward a far-off goal and following one's innate faith in life

Trust in a larger order is aided by an optimistic, philosophical orientation

Need to take advantage of opportunities for outer and inner exploration in order to improve self

Too much expansion can lead to over-extension of energy and overlooking the immediate possibilities

Has an innate well-developed appreciation of the importance of the religious dimension of life

Interpretive Guidelines for Jupiter in Capricorn:

Seeks to grow and improve oneself through hard work, discipline, and steady progress

Need to express qualities of self-control and confident conservatism in order to improve self; has innate sense of authority that inspires trust from other people

Optimism and expansion can be squelched by an overly serious, fearful attitude

One's faith and trust is based on reality, experience, and one's innate understanding of the value of history and tradition

Opportunities come through one's ability to be reliable, responsible, and patient—qualities that are usually well-developed

Interpretive Guidelines for Jupiter in Aquarius:

Seeks to grow and improve oneself through humanitarian ideals, intellectual development, and daring experimentation

♃ Optimism can be deflected by an overly-detached, uninvolved attitude, but usually generous toward others

♒ Need to feel completely independent intellectually in order to have full confidence in self; has a well-developed scientific attitude by nature

One's faith is eccentric, individualistic, unorthodox, and unique to oneself

Trusts in the unity of all humanity and all knowledge, and has a broad tolerance for a wide variety of free expression

Interpretive Guidelines for Jupiter in Pisces:

♃ Seeks to grow and improve oneself through living one's ideals, expanding one's sympathies, and generosity of spirit

♓ Need to be compassionate and sensitive in order to feel faith in oneself

Acting on the need for self-improvement can be hindered by unfocused, noncritical attitudes and escapism

Openness to grace is based on one's compassion toward all that suffers

Has a well-developed trust in a higher power; understands the importance of devotion to an ideal and openness to the spiritual dimension of experience

Saturn in the Signs—
Interpretive Guidelines

THE SIGN POSITION OF SATURN: How one seeks to establish & preserve self through effort

Interpretive Guidelines for Saturn in Aries:

♄ Seeks to establish and preserve self through an energetic push toward new experience

♈ Dynamic effort is focused toward a single-pointed release of energy; develops self by cultivating courage and daring

Urge for tangible achievement through aggressive, competitive actions

Acceptance of responsibility can be hindered by childish, egocentric attitude, or freedom of action can be hindered by fear and excessive caution

Acting independently is especially important and necessary for satisfying achievement

Interpretive Guidelines for Saturn in Taurus:

♄ Seeks to establish and preserve self through steady productivity, ownership, and reliance on one's own material resources

♉ One's integrity and security are based on loyalty, stability, and reliability, but achievement could be hindered by laziness

Feels need to focus on basic (often traditional) values in order to attain social approval

Urge to consolidate and possess can lead to blockage of energy flow—an extremely conservative and unyielding stubbornness with a fear of losing control

Capable of diligent effort toward deepening appreciation of physical sensations, art, beauty, or nature

Interpretive Guidelines for Saturn in Gemini:

♄ Seeks to establish and preserve self through perceptive abilities and command of facts

♊ A need to rely on one's own mental resources leads to constant restructuring of one's thought processes

Acceptance of duties and responsibilities can be blocked by a need for varied mental stimulation; ability to learn and experiment open-mindedly can be hindered by skeptical attitudes and unnecessarily narrow interests

One needs to focus in a disciplined way on expressing ideas coherently and thinking objectively

Urge to intellectualize and verbally defend one's structure and integrity

Interpretive Guidelines for Saturn in Cancer:

♄ Seeks to establish and preserve self through feelings of deep nurturing and through clarifying familial roots and influences

♋ Accepting one's emotions and expressing them in a focused way is especially important, although often quite difficult

One puts effort into overcoming fear of one's own sensitivity and vulnerability

Strong urge toward achieving self-protection to enhance safety and security

Too much restraint put on emotions can lead to rigidity and hollowness

Interpretive Guidelines for Saturn in Leo:

♄ Seeks to establish and preserve self through creative activity, self-expression, and loyal, disciplined affection

♌ Urge to focus one's individuality into achievement in order to attain a sense of security

Need to rely on and trust one's inner soul attunement and one's deepest heartfelt concerns

Fear and lack of trust in one's innate value and goodness can hinder self-expression and self-confidence

Pride and urge for recognition are factors in one's acceptance of duties and responsibilities, and creatively handling responsibilities can produce deep happiness

Interpretive Guidelines for Saturn in Virgo:

♄ Seeks to establish and preserve self through one's analytical abilities, handling of responsibilities dutifully, and by being helpful to those in need

♍ Organization and discipline are aimed toward mastering details and perfecting skills and lead to deep satisfaction

Lack of faith in one's ability to work effectively with the physical world can lead to self-doubt and excessive fears

A need to put concentrated effort into working efficiently produces real achievement

Reliance upon one's own helpfulness and technical ability leads to establishment of a secure place in the world and developing true humility

Interpretive Guidelines for Saturn in Libra:

♄ Seeks to establish and preserve self through ability to relate to others fairly and responsibly

♎ Consciously organizes schedules, relationships, and all structures upon principles of balance and harmony

Fear of committed partnership can hinder achievement and prevent a sense of satisfying intimacy

Disciplined effort is put into maintaining relationships; all commitments, promises, and duties are honored and can bring deep satisfaction

Desire to please other people can inhibit acceptance of distasteful duties, but tactfulness and impartiality can bring social approval

Interpretive Guidelines for Saturn in Scorpio:

♄ ♏ Seeks to establish and preserve self through control of powerful passions and other reserves of energy

Strong urge to defend one's emotional structure, which can even lead to undermining one's goals or blocking intimacy with others

An obsessive need to rely on one's own resources can interfere with broader achievement

Fear of expressing or even acknowledging the deepest emotions can lead to rigidity, a "frozen" flow of feelings, and lack of deep satisfaction in life

Disciplined effort is exerted toward total transformation, elimination of all that's unnecessary, and often on significant reform work

Interpretive Guidelines for Saturn in Sagittarius:

♄ ♐ Seeks to establish and preserve self through firm beliefs and aspirations toward distant goals

Can expansively accept many duties and responsibilities, often taking on more than one can handle; strong need for mental discipline

Organizes "on the run," constantly changing schedules and structures to suit a situation; having a systematic approach to future achievements is especially important

Effort is put into philosophical pursuits and clearly formulating one's ideals, which can produce a sense of security and satisfaction

Strong need to seek social approval for one's beliefs; free pursuit of truth may be hindered by overly traditional attitudes or other fears

Interpretive Guidelines for Saturn in Capricorn:

Seeks to establish and preserve self through attainment of one's ambitions, authority, and position in society

♄ Strongly disciplined effort expended toward planning the
♑ fulfillment of one's responsibilities

♑ Overly-developed organizing ability can lead to attempts to
control all situations too tightly

Urge to defend self's structure and integrity through determination, hard work, conservatism, and cautious behavior;
excessive fear of disapproval can hinder the full achievement of one's aims

Deep-seated need to be a reliable person and to depend on
one's own resources

Interpretive Guidelines for Saturn in Aquarius:

♄ Seeks to establish and preserve self through disciplined men-
♒ tal abilities, clearly defined knowledge, and commitment
♒ to social or futuristic goals

♒ Well-developed ability to organize groups of people and/or
concepts

Effort is expended toward maintaining a circle of important
friendships, often guiding this group energy toward specific achievements

Urge toward eccentricity and extremism can jeopardize
chances for tangible achievement, and free, independent
self-expression can be hindered by mental rigidity or social
insecurity

Need to interact socially in order to stabilize one's purpose
in life and to overcome fear of disapproval

Interpretive Guidelines for Saturn in Pisces:

♄ Seeks to establish and preserve self through transcending per-
♓ sonality limitations and uniting with a greater being,
♓ group, or ideal

♓ Yearning for an escape from reality can delay or interfere with
one's acceptance of duties and responsibilities, or excessive
fearfulness or conservatism can thwart the realization of
transcendent visions

Healing compassion and empathy are expressed through disciplined effort, and rigidity is dissolved through this giving effort

A need to express one's sensitivity and emotions and to discipline one's evasiveness in order to feel stable

Need to rely upon one's own spiritual resources by making one's higher vision and yearning practical

Uranus, Neptune & Pluto
in the Signs

Although the sign positions of Uranus, Neptune, and Pluto are significant as indicators of generational qualities (explaining many differences in mass psychology from era to era), they are in themselves relatively unimportant for individuals. They do not represent *clearly individualized qualities*, since they remain in one sign for many years. The house positions and the aspects of these planets are invariably more significant for individuals than the sign positions. The aspects to the personal planets by Uranus, Neptune, and Pluto can sometimes reveal how one is attuned to the forces of change within his or her generation, although the outer three planets do seem to be "silent notes" in some people's lives, and the profound changes that they represent can for other people take place solely on inner, personal levels. The interests and activities of the individual must be related to the chart in order to see how the other planets are being expressed.

In other words, the *sign* qualities and energies denoted by outer planets' positions are not usually much in evidence in individuals (unless they are closely tied into the rest of the chart's major factors in a powerful way). For example, Uranus, Neptune, or Pluto could amplify a sign's energies considerably if in a conjunction with one of the other seven planets in that sign. (E.g., Pluto conjunct Venus in Leo would amplify the Leo energy in the individual.) One of the outer planets can also further emphasize a particular *element* if it is in trine aspect to two planets in the other two signs of that element (that is, if it is part of a "Grand Trine" configuration, such as Uranus in Gemini trine Sun in Aquarius and Moon in Libra—hence Uranus amplifies the Air element energy).

Another example of an instance where the sign energies would be amplified by the presence of an outer planet in that sign is any time the Rising Sign contains Uranus, Neptune, or

Pluto. Even if the outer planet is on the Twelfth House side of the Ascendant, it is safe to say that the Rising Sign's qualities are significantly augmented. An example would be Pluto in Leo with Leo Rising; the Leo qualities would be strengthened, although very likely held in to some extent due to Pluto's secretiveness and self-control.

CHAPTER 6

THE ASCENDANT (OR RISING SIGN) & THE MIDHEAVEN

Key Concepts for the Ascendant

The Ascendant (or "Rising Sign"*) is almost impossible to sum up. It is many things at once: a symbol of how one *acts* in the world, the "mask" or "image of the personality" that others see, and a spontaneous energy and attitude toward life that pervades the entire being. Although in some people it is quite obvious, the Ascendant can also be, as Dane Rudhyar wrote, "the most elusive and hard-to-know factor in a birth chart." In some people it appears to be primarily a superficial quality, as expressed in this quotation from Jeff Mayo:

> It can be the face a man wears whilst he projects himself into his business and social activities, concealing much of his true character that only his intimates—and often not even they—know exists.

---

*Although the terms "Ascendant" and "Rising Sign" are usually used interchangeably, there is a distinction. The Ascendant (often abbreviated ASC) technically is the exact degree of the Rising Sign on the eastern horizon in a birth chart and hence a more precise term. The Rising Sign is simply the sign that was "rising" over the eastern horizon at birth.

And yet, this "image of the personality" that others see is not intentionally projected; it is automatic. Furthermore, neither is it superficial in the sense that many astrological writings imply. The Ascendant always indicates something essential about the person that is at once deeply inner and also outer. It is virtually impossible for a person to act in the world or express himself or herself without bringing the Ascendant into play. In many ways, it is the gate through which we most directly confront the outer world. It symbolizes our individual *approach* to life itself. It represents the way one actively merges with life in the outer world when one's energy is flowing spontaneously.

The Ascendant reveals the way we feel ourselves to be uniquely ourselves. It always denotes something essential about the individual's personality and approach to life, but it may appear more dominant and authentic when the rest of the chart supports and harmonizes with it. When the rest of the chart is not particularly attuned to the qualities and energy of the Ascendant, the ASC may then appear more superficial, a relatively artificial mask that may be quite at odds with the rest of the person's nature.

The Element of the Ascendant

The element of the Ascendant reveals the quality of energy flow directly vitalizing the physical body and the overall approach to life.* Fire or Air signs rising tend to conduct energy, encouraging active *self-expression* and dynamic expenditure of energy. Earth or Water signs rising tend to conserve and resist the flow of vital energies, and hence indicate *self-containment* (sometimes *self-repression*) and the tendency of living within oneself.

Fire Signs Rising (Aries, Leo, & Sagittarius):
Great vitality, physically energetic, beams energy outward into the world. Marked by a positive, optimistic outlook on life and a confident, bluntly honest demeanor. Active, wants to make a mark on life and see the results of one's efforts manifested in the world. Action-orientation can lead to wasteful excesses and less awareness of the subtler needs of self and others.

Air Signs Rising (Gemini, Libra, & Aquarius):
Mentally quick and active; inquisitive, social, friendly, verbal. Often clever, with rapid perceptions. Can be overly intellectual to the point of chronically debating everything inwardly without taking action. Wants to *understand* everything; lives a lot in the world of concepts. Has a natural facility for communication and perceiving others' viewpoints.

Earth Signs Rising (Taurus, Virgo, & Capricorn):
A matter-of-fact outlook. Focus on the material world and conservative attitudes can inhibit imagination, which is then allowed to limit the person's options and/or restrain spontaneous self-expression. Steadiness and reliability are often well-developed and highly valued by self and others. Practicality and inborn patience give more tolerance for routine than

---

*See also page 173 ff. of the author's *New Insights in Modern Astrology: The Jupiter/Saturn Conference Lectures*, also published by CRCS Publications.

other Ascendants show. A systematic approach, usually along established channels, is the most common method of expressing oneself.

Water Signs Rising (Cancer, Scorpio, & Pisces):
Most easily influenced by the environment and by other people. Sensitive, moody, wary because of a strong feeling of vulnerability and likelihood of being hurt. Protective of self but also of others one cares about. Sympathetic, feels others' emotions immediately and forcefully. Very private, lives deeply within oneself.

The Ruler of the Ascendant

The planet that is associated with the Rising Sign is so important that it has been known traditionally as the "Ruler of the Chart"* or the birth chart's "Ruling Planet." By its sign and house position, it invariably colors the individual's entire approach to life. Once you have tuned in on and accepted the field of experience and the type of energy represented by the ruling planet and its house and sign, you begin to feel more alive, more motivated to express yourself, and more inwardly secure and true to yourself.

Ruling Planet's Sign Position: Reveals an energy attunement and specific qualities that are powerfully important and even dominant in many cases. This sign shows a primary motivating energy in the person's actions and self-expression.

Ruling Planet's House Position: Shows a field of experience where much of one's life energy and effort manifest, and where one will encounter life activities and issues that are deeply important. One must be active in this area of life in order to express and stimulate many essential energies and abilities.

Actually, the ASC and its ruling planet must always be considered together, as one interpretive unit. For example, a Gemini Rising with Ruling Planet Mercury in Pisces will usually be

---

*If your Ascendant is one of those which has both an ancient ruler and a modern ruler, such as Scorpio, Pisces, and Aquarius, you should look at the house positions of both of them, for both will be at least somewhat emphasized in the person's life. However, look especially to the *ancient ruler's sign position* because that sign will always be much stronger than the sign of the modern ruler, assuming other emphases are not present. For example, if you have Scorpio rising, your Mars sign is generally much more important in your personal make-up than is your Pluto sign, unless another major factor is in the Pluto sign. With the Pluto in Leo generation, for instance, not every one of them with Scorpio rising is particularly Leonine in their individual nature and personality. But in every case of Scorpio rising, the Mars sign is especially powerful; that energy flows assertively through them in every case; that energy is projected with special emphasis in every one of them.

more imaginative, psychically sensitive, and absent-mindedly confused than a Gemini Rising with Mercury in Taurus, where the mind will function more slowly and practically. [I call these Gemini Rising with a Pisces "Subtone" and Gemini Rising with a Taurus "Subtone."] For another example, a Cancer Rising with Ruling Planet Moon in Libra is likely to be more detached and more diplomatic than Cancer Rising with Moon in Aries, which is so impulsive and often tactless. (I would call these two examples a Cancer Rising with a Libra "Subtone" and a Cancer Rising with an Aries "Subtone.")

Aspects to the Ascendant

[NOTE: The birth time must be reliable to use these aspects.]

The Ascendant's tone is modified not only by the position of its ruling planet, but also by *any* close 30°-multiple angle (or "aspect") to the Ascendant by any planet.* The planet aspecting the Ascendant always makes a dynamic impact and always affects the image of the personality that is projected and the entire mode of self-expression. Any such planet strongly colors the person's energy field and attitude toward life itself.

a) Conjunctions to the Ascendant, within 6°, are the most powerful of these aspects and the most immediately noticeable qualities in the person's personality.

b) Conjunctions to the Descendant, within 6° (that is, oppositions to the Ascendant), are the second most powerful of these aspects. Since the ASC shows the most immediate image a person projects, whereas the DSC and planets near it show qualities that especially emerge in relationships and may be contrary to the person's image, these aspects can sometimes indicate an inner division in the individual, wherein the person alternately manifests two different modes of being that seem completely opposite, symbolized by the ASC and the planet opposite it. In other cases, there seems to be simply a strong coloration of the personality by that planet, particularly seen in the area of personal relationships, with no significant opposite or contradictory problems being felt.

c) Square aspects to the Ascendant are often among the most frustrating or challenging of aspects to the ASC. They sometimes symbolize pressures from the person's early environment, manifesting as a type of oppression or inhibition (especially when the planet involved is in the 4th house), or

---

*I consider all the 30°-multiple aspects to be "major aspects": 30°, 60°, 90°, 120°, 150°, and 180°. See Chapter 8 for more details on each aspect's specific meaning.

as a pressure toward achievement or recognition (especially when the planet involved is in the 10th house). However, like all such challenging aspects, these squares can also show where the greatest effort toward growth may take place.

d) Any planet closely aspecting the Ascendant adds its quality to your consciousness, starting at an early age.* You have it within you and at your disposal automatically, *although you may have to learn to acknowledge or integrate it.* In other words, you can consciously develop that quality further as time goes by. It can be a major source of energy for you once you learn to tap it.

e) Even if the Sun and Moon make no close aspect with the Ascendant, and even if the birth time is slightly in doubt, it is still very important to understand how the *elements* of these three dominant factors blend within the individual. This will clarify how the essential energies of life flow together and to what extent the Ascendant encourages or restrains the expression of the Sun and Moon energies.

---

*See Chapter 8 of this book for guidelines to interpreting each specific planet's aspects with the Ascendant.

Guidelines to
Interpreting the Ascendant

Although the Ascendant is of deep and pervasive importance for each individual, there is no denying that it must be related to the rest of the chart,* and especially to the Sun Sign, in order to understand it thoroughly for a particular person. The Sun, after all, is the core identity, the very center of the consciousness, the way we assimilate much of our experience, whereas the Ascendant—although it varies in importance from person to person—is not as central to the person's nature. It shows, among other things, the approach to life; but the Sun shows life itself! The Ascendant must serve the purposes, values, and creative goals of the Sun for the individual to function happily and fully.

The Ascendant modifies the expression of the Solar energy. An entire book could be written studying the interplay of all the combinations of Sun and Ascendant, but just to give an example, a Gemini rising will always give a more socially lively and intellectually curious approach to life to *any* Sun Sign. It will even speed up a slow Taurus Sun, make a Scorpio Sun more social and less secretive, help a Capricorn Sun to be less defensive and more communicative, and encourage a Cancer Sun to be less shy! And yet, in all cases, no matter how similar all these Gemini rising people may seem in approach and observable personality, the central nature shown by the Sun remains defined by the Sun's sign position.

Another useful tool for understanding how a person's Ascendant and Sun Sign interact is to compare the elements of the two factors. For example, a Cancer Sun Sign person with a Fire sign rising is usually far more extroverted, forcefully expressive, and

---

*Also see Chapter 10 of *Astrology, Karma & Transformation* for more information on how to understand the Ascendant and its relationship to the rest of the chart. That chapter also includes significant material on the Midheaven.

confident than a Cancer Sun individual with, say, a more conservative, self-protective Earth sign rising. For another example, an Air sign Sun person with a Water sign rising may appear much more emotional than he or she really is, whereas a Water sign Sun person with an Air sign rising may appear far more detached and less emotional than he or she is.

The Sun in a sign always brings forth a strongly energized manifestation of that sign; although aspects to the Sun add a modifying tone to the Solar expression, one's Sun Sign energy will hardly ever be as thoroughly altered as that of the Rising Sign can be. The Rising Sign often contains no planet, and even when it does contain a planet or two, it cannot be equal in power to the sign that contains the Sun itself (unless of course one has the Sun Sign rising!). The Ascendant qualities are thus far more easily modified, in most cases, than are the qualities and energies of the Sun Sign. Close aspects to the Ascendant strongly modify its expression, and the Sign position and aspects of the Ascendant's ruling planet have a profound impact on the expression of the Rising Sign's energies.

The resulting complexity of the Ascendant factor explains many things. It explains why some people do not identify very much with their Rising Sign. It explains why new students of astrology often have a hard time grasping the concept and interpretation of the Ascendant. It explains how it is that many central characteristics and tendencies of a given individual are not immediately apparent in the symbolism of the Sun and Rising Signs, and thus why many people simply do not see much immediate usefulness in basic astrological "labels."

It should also be pointed out that people are often relatively unaware of their Ascendant nature, as compared to their Sun Sign. In that sense, the Ascendant is a factor that can be consciously developed further over time and consciously utilized to aid one's self-expression. I have known people who were relieved to find what their Rising Signs were, since it finally gave them a way of identifying a very deep but only semi-conscious tendency in themselves. In some cases, the qualities and abilities symbolized by the Ascendant were just beginning to emerge, and learning the astrological keys to this factor helped personal development greatly. (I should emphasize here that, perhaps more than with most other factors in the chart, the early environment can encourage or suppress the expression of the Ascendant's energies, since it is a primary channel with which one interacts with the outer world.)

Keeping in mind that the Ascendant is quite readily modified by the ruling planet's position and by aspects to the Ascendant (as well as by 1st House planets), we can make a few general observations about the twelve different Ascendants. The reader should also use the interpretive guidelines for "The Sun in the Signs" in Chapter 5 to further explore the essential nature of each Ascendant. Newer students especially are encouraged to utilize that section for interpretive help with the various Rising Signs. I find that those guidelines for the Sun work quite well when applied to the Ascendant, and therefore, rather than repeating those key phrases in the following paragraphs, I will try to approach the meaning of each Ascendant from another angle.

In the following notes, I often use the widely accepted abbreviation for the Ascendant, ASC, for brevity. Here and there in the following, I have also mentioned various significant contrasts between the Sun Sign and the same sign on the Ascendant which I have observed over the past twenty years. These observations are admittedly subjective and may not apply to every case that the reader may know of. But I feel that the value of stimulating thought and perhaps even controversy is a more useful learning method than simply listing endless adjectives for each Ascendant. The reader should view the following comparative evaluations as guidelines, and as questions to explore, rather than as rigid statements of absolute truth.

ARIES ASCENDANT: Abrupt, ambitious, restless, impatient, always in a hurry to rush through life, these people can be quite abrasive. If Mars is in Pisces, Cancer, or one of the Earth signs, these forceful qualities can be somewhat moderated.

The blunt directness of Aries Sun that can seem so offensive, insensitive, and inconsiderate to others is often toned down in many people with Aries ASC. Nonetheless, the enterprising spirit of Aries is still there, sometimes even more dynamically than in many people with Aries Sun.

TAURUS ASCENDANT: Methodical, controlled, measured movements that often seem like holding a pose; deep dislike of being rushed, strong aesthetic and pleasure-motivated streak in the nature. Can be lazy or steadily productive, but still insists on doing everything in one's own way and at one's own pace. Venus' sign position strongly affects how ambitious or dynamic the person is. Taurus Sun more often seems lazy than Taurus ASC (probably because the Sun is the essential vital energy), and Taurus Sun also seems to be more predictably possessive. Both want to *enjoy* everything they do, and therefore they refuse to rush anything, lest they interfere with the pleasure they are deriving from the here and now. An extremely physical and sensual approach to life, and a strong need for closeness, affection, and security.

GEMINI ASCENDANT: The most inquisitive and friendly Rising Sign, but also the one most inclined to be worried about oneself all the time (except perhaps Libra rising in some cases). Usually very intelligent and curious, and has a tremendous need to communicate verbally. The superficiality so often seen in Gemini Sun is not usually as evident in the Gemini Ascendant, but the tendency for one side of the mind not to know what the other side thinks or says is often even more extreme in the Gemini ASC—which can be most infuriating to those who would like to rely on the person and believe what he/she says. The person is not intentionally dishonest; it is just that the right hand knows not what the left hand is doing! (I should also state, however, that I have encountered at least two Gemini Rising people who are very reliable!)

CANCER ASCENDANT: A sympathetic, mild demeanor, but the sensitivity and sympathy are often directed just as much toward oneself as toward others, often being *oversensitive* to hurts and slights. In this sense, Cancer Rising seems to exhibit a more superficial type of empathy for others than Cancer Sun, whose feelings tend to go deeper and whose sentiment is more personally touching. Cancer ASC often seems even more reserved and private than the Cancer Sun person, who by virtue of his or her great acting ability can often seem quite social and outgoing. The Cancer Rising person is usually a strong introvert, although I have seen cases where the Moon was in Leo or a similar extroverted sign and the more outward-oriented tendencies were predominant.

LEO ASCENDANT: A Leo Ascendant often seems to motivate a person to try hard to express one's best self. That is not to say that the pride (and even arrogance) of the sign Leo is completely absent from those with Leo Rising, but it does appear that they have less need to "lord it over" other people than those with Leo Sun do. The Leo ASC seems to encourage an especially authentic expression of the person's Sun energy, whereas the Leo Sun person often displays a more self-conscious dramatization of his or her deeper feelings. Bigheartedness, often said to be a trait of Leo, seems to be a more reliable quality in those with Leo ASC than Leo Sun, which so often insensitively manipulates others for personal gain. Leo ASC can, however, demonstrate an extremely aloof bearing and, because of their inordinate need for respect and a show of dignity, often seems to lack the spontaneous humor and playfulness of Leo Sun.

VIRGO ASCENDANT: Virgo ASC people often have a higher level of self-confidence than Virgo Sun people, and oddly enough, their humility often seems more authentic in at least one way: those with Virgo ASC always acknowledge that they have more to learn and further to go to improve themselves. The self-criticism that so often defeats and depresses Virgo Sun people is sometimes, but not nearly so often, found in the Virgo ASC. It is as if the Virgo ASC more often "works off" their doubts rather than just dwelling on them. The conservative and conventional qualities found in abundance in Virgo Sun are not nearly so deep-seated in the Virgo rising person, who may appear aloof, severe, or withdrawn but whose appearance may hide a much wilder nature. The Virgo Sun person is usually better with detailed analysis than is the Virgo ASC, although both often display craftmanship skills.

LIBRA ASCENDANT: Although a Libra ASC often tends toward a somewhat narcissistic self-centeredness more often than is the case with Libra Sun, it must be stated also that the Libra ASC person is sometimes genuinely kinder and sweeter than is the Libra Sun, who often relates to others in a more detached way, realizing that life is not all sweetness and light. Libra Rising lends a personal tone to the way all the other energies of the chart are expressed. Although close relationships are of central importance to those with Libra Sun, the need for "the other" is sometimes even more crucial for the Libra ASC person, whose entire life often seems focused on the primary relationship of their life (or the lack of such a relationship). When there is no partner, the Libra ASC person sometimes loses all sense of direction and can feel a serious lack of initiative and physical energy. Fuller details about their relationship needs can be understood by evaluating Venus in the chart. The Libra ASC individual often at least *appears* more superficial than the Libra Sun, who is usually much deeper than they let on. Also, Libra ASC seems to retain a romantic view of life longer than the often cynical Libra Sun.

SCORPIO ASCENDANT: Always known for intensity, those with Scorpio Rising are very often associated with the healing arts, exploring other people's motives (such as through psychotherapy), or exploring the unknown or esoteric. Although Scorpio is often described as courageous, what is usually not mentioned is how much fear is the element motivating their actions. For Scorpio, the best defense is a good offense. Those with Scorpio Rising are constantly on the defensive to a degree not usually seen in Scorpio Sun. Scorpio is a sign of emotional extremism, and it is therefore easy to find a powerful negative expression of Scorpio ASC for every positive expression. Scorpio Rising has in fact gained a rather negative reputation over the years, one which is not entirely undeserved. No other Rising Sign can rival it for vindictive, ruthless, jealous behavior. Vengeance is often a strong motivating factor in their behavior, as is a sometimes paranoid obsession with self-preservation. This often takes the form of a reluctance to let go of anything—money or emotions; they have a great fear of letting go and losing control. Those with Scorpio ASC can be perceptive into others' deeper feelings and motives, when not projecting their own motives onto others. They can be extremely resourceful and often intensely dedicated to a difficult challenge or life mission. The negative traits mentioned above are sometimes greatly ameliorated in Scorpio Sun people, who can be very loyal to those whom they allow into their "inner circle" of friends. Also, the tendency to undermine oneself seems much less common in Scorpio Sun than in Scorpio ASC. In considering the ruling planet of the ASC, the Mars sign is always more important than the sign of Pluto, and a positively directed Mars can help channel and transform the often self-destructive Scorpio energy.

SAGITTARIUS ASCENDANT: The optimism, buoyancy, enthusiasm, and broad-mindedness that are often, but not always, seen in Sagittarius Sun people are almost uniformly expressed by those who have Sagittarius ASC. Virtually every Sagittarius ASC person I have ever seen could be described as perpetually "up beat," even in the face of continued disappointments or obstacles. Although the tendency toward forcefully preaching one's personal beliefs as universal truth is present in Sagittarius ASC as well as in Sagittarius Sun, the ASC expression of this tendency is usually more tolerant and inspiring, while the preaching of a Sagittarius Sun person is often experienced as being hit over the head with "the Truth." In other words, self-righteousness seems considerably more flagrant in those with Sun in Sagittarius. Also, Sagittarius ASC people almost never show the aimless, drifting discontent that is so often seen in those with Sagittarius Sun. Sagittarius Rising seems more inclined toward definite action in line with an ideal, whereas Sagittarius Sun is sometimes limited to mental or theoretical activity alone.

CAPRICORN ASCENDANT: Capricorn Rising often expresses itself with extreme negativity and skepticism, more often than Capricorn Sun does. However, one should understand that in both cases this apparent cynicism and disdain for the new is often a protective cover for a more inquisitive, vulnerable, even spiritually-open nature. Capricorn simply does not like to have time wasted on unproven ideas, but practical and logical proof even of unorthodox realities will often be enough to capture their interest and eliminate their automatic skepticism. Although Capricorn Sun and ASC are both extremely concerned with outer form, appearances, and reputation, the Capricorn ASC seems to be far more fearful of public opinion, often going to great lengths to appear normal, conservative, and "safe." Capricorn Sun seems to have a greater drive toward achievement and authority and a more determined approach to worldly success. Capricorn ASC sometimes seems satisfied merely with being secure. Both are so impersonal that relations with others are often problematical, although Capricorn Sun more often than Capricorn ASC finds it hard to relate on an even one-to-one level.

AQUARIUS ASCENDANT: An unconventional, rebellious streak pervades the personalities of both Aquarius ASC and Aquarius Sun people, but these traits go much deeper in those with Aquarius Sun. They are usually lifelong afficionados of the new, the imaginative, and the revolutionary, even if they don't express it overtly very often. Those with Aquarius Rising often seem a bit kooky; indeed, they often feel rebellious, but there is usually a stronger attunement to convention in them than is seen in most Aquarius Sun individuals. Both types usually exhibit an immediacy of perception and understanding, a thinking speed and rapidity of learning, that can be startling to their slower friends. Both exhibit a cold detachment that is frustrating and often shocking to more emotionally sensitive people; Sun in Aquarius seems to be more aloof and impersonal than is Aquarius ASC. The traditional Saturn rulership seems to be stronger than the modern ruler Uranus in many people who have Aquarius Rising. But the house and sign position of Saturn is always important for *all* Aquarius ASC people.

PISCES ASCENDANT: Because the Sun is weak in Pisces, thus allowing Pisces Sun individuals to be strongly influenced by all of the other factors in their charts, there seem to be more types of Pisces Sun individuals than Pisces Rising people. Those with Pisces ASC are almost uniformly sensitive, compassionate, emotional, imaginative, and helpful. There seems to be a strength of character in the Pisces ASC that is sometimes lacking in the Pisces Sun, who is so often passive, evasive, escapist, and irresponsible. Probably it is the ancient ruler of Pisces, Jupiter, that accounts for the strength of character and buoyancy that is especially evident in so many Pisces ASC people; sometimes that is far more apparent than the influence of the modern ruler Neptune. In fact, one should always look to the Jupiter sign and house of Pisces ASC people for key insights to their nature. Besides being able to empathize with and help those who are having difficulties, Pisces Rising people are also often philosophical and surprisingly unperturbed when they themselves experience misfortune. Like Virgo ASC (its opposite sign), Pisces ASC people don't feel the need for credit or public acknowledgement for all they contribute to others.

The Midheaven

Aging and maturing often mean reaching for and concretiz-
ing the goals and dreams that we envision when we are young.
The Midheaven's sign, the placement of its ruler, and planets
in the 10th house symbolize this process. Although the Midheaven sign is not always obvious in an outward way, it is always
an important part of the birth chart, since it describes the
manifestation and development of one's vocation and standing
in the world. Almost all astrological texts describe the Midheaven
(or MC as it is often abbreviated) as representing one's ''career''
or ''place in the world.'' It is those things, as well as a few others.
When young, a person does not usually identify with the type
of energy represented by the sign on the MC, unless one or more
of the personal planets are in that sign also. The Midheaven symbolizes qualities that we spontaneously grow toward as we get
older, qualities that require effort to attain. It represents achievement, authority, your potential social contribution, and your
vocation or ''calling.'' Fulfillment comes through learning to express the energy represented by the sign on the MC.

The Ruling Planet of the Midheaven

The ruling planet of the Midheaven sign is important not
only due to its general symbolic meaning, but also due to the
fact that *its house position so often shows where your real vocation comes into clearest focus.* That house represents a field of
experience which feels like your true calling at a very deep level.
If your Midheaven is in a sign that has a traditional ruler and
a modern ruler, the house position of both can be important.
However, the sign position of the traditional ruler is usually more
important than that of the modern ruler.

Planets in the 10th House
& Aspects to the Midheaven

Planets in the 10th house, especially those that conjunct the MC (on *either side of the MC*), represent ways of being, qualities, and types of activity that are extremely *important* to the individual and which he or she respects. Due to this feeling of respect, people will often exhibit these qualities or express these energies publicly in order that others might think well of them.

Other than the conjunction, other close aspects to the Midheaven can be considered almost equal in effect. The type of aspect is much less important than the specific planet making that aspect, and the exactitude of the aspect. Traditionally, these aspects are correlated with your public self-expression, career, and vocational goals. Any planet in *close* aspect with the Midheaven indicates a type of energy and orientation which is essential in the achievement of your position in the world and instrumental in what you will contribute to society.

For example, with Venus closely aspecting the Midheaven, it is important to contribute something artistic or beautiful to society. One-to-one interactions are likely to be important to one's public self-expression, and the person is likely to be concerned with making a pleasant and cooperative contribution to society.

As another example, in the charts of three publishers I can think of off hand, Jupiter is in a very close aspect to the MC in all three charts: the conjunction in one and the sextile in the other two. And traditionally, Jupiter is the planet of publishing.

THE BLIND SPOT

*Originally published in July, 1943. Excerpted from *Astrology, Science of Prediction* by Sidney K. Bennett, Wynn Publishing Co., Los Angeles, CA, 1945.

CHAPTER 7
THE HOUSES—
INTERPRETIVE GUIDELINES

The houses represent the *fields of* experience wherein the energies of the signs and planets operate. Rather than symbolizing just the outward experiences and environmental circumstances specified by most traditional astrology, the houses are also revealing of the inner state and of one's personal subjective experience and attitudes. By noting the planets' placements in the natal chart, an astrologer can tell which levels and areas of experience will be strongly emphasized in a person's life. The keyword system discussed on the following pages is meant to clarify interpretation and understanding primarily of the psychological and inner significance of the houses. It is an attempt to perceive the *essential* meanings of the fields of experience known as the "houses." If the essential meanings are understood, they can then be applied to and illuminate all the diverse activities and experiences traditionally symbolized by the houses.

The Wholistic Approach to Interpreting Houses

Emphasizing the *type of house* containing planets in a natal chart helps one to see the chart as a whole. One familiar way of defining the houses is to separate them into the classifications of *angular, succedent,* and *cadent.*

The **angular** houses (1, 4, 7, 10) are associated with a self-activating quality and have an immediate impact on the structure of one's life. The keyword for the angular houses is **ACTION.**

The **succedent** houses (2, 5, 8, 11) are associated with individual desires and the areas of life we want to control and consolidate. The keyword for this type of house is **SECURITY.**

The **cadent** houses (3, 6, 9, 12) are areas where there is input, exchange, and distribution of thoughts and observations. The keyword for these houses is **LEARNING.**

The progression of houses from angular through succedent and cadent and back to angular again symbolizes the flow of life experience: we act, we consolidate the results of our actions in order to gain security, we learn from what we have done and become aware of what remains to be done; and therefore, we act again. Thus, a person with a strong emphasis on one of these three types of houses by planetary placement invariably pours a lot of energy into and experiences many challenges related to action, security, or learning.

The houses can also be divided into groups of three, depending upon the element of the signs associated with that group of houses. Key phrases and guidelines for understanding these groups are as follows. [Please note that the terms "Psychic Trinity," "Trinity of Wealth," etc. are quite old terms, and are used here primarily as convenient labels.]

WATER HOUSES ("THE PSYCHIC TRINITY"—4, 8, 12): All of these houses deal with the past, with the conditioned responses that are now instinctual and operate through the emotions. Planets in these houses show what is happening on subconscious levels and indicate the process of gaining consciousness through the *assimilation* of the essence of the past, while simultaneously letting go of the useless memories and fears that hold us back. The person with an emphasis on these houses lives a great deal in the feelings and in his or her deeper YEARNINGS. The emotional and soul needs dominate much of the person's life activity and energy expenditure. Planets in the water houses affect the individual's emotional predisposition, how he or she copes with fulfilling private needs and confronting obsessive feelings, and to what extent the person lives in a private way or in the inner life. The keywords for the water houses are **EMOTIONAL** and **SOUL**.

EARTH HOUSES ("THE TRINITY OF WEALTH"—2, 6, 10): These houses are associated with the level of experience wherein we try to satisfy our basic NEEDS in the practical world. Planets in these houses indicate energies that can most easily be put to use in dealing with the physical world, and that can be developed as expertise in management of resources. The person with an emphasis on these houses lives energetically in the physical world, building, doing, achieving, acquiring, and defining his or her purpose in life by the status and security achieved. Those with a strong emphasis in the earth houses tend to want to settle into a niche in life, as they are searching for the place where they can be the most productive and most easily satisfy their practical needs. This person experiences self most immediately through work, through feeling useful, and through practical achievement. He or she wants to fulfill a calling or role in the great world outside. Planets in the earth houses affect the individual's attitudes toward vocation, career ambitions, and the capacity to produce effective results. The keyword for these houses is **MATERIAL,** for the earth houses deal chiefly with concerns of the material world.

FIRE HOUSES ("THE TRINITY OF LIFE"—1, 5, 9): These houses are associated with one's attitude toward life and the experience of being alive. They represent an outpouring of energy into the world and the *aspirations* and *inspirations* that motivate us to do so. The person with an emphasis on these houses lives in his or her enthusiasms, ideals, and dreams for the future. Faith and confidence (or the marked lack of it) and the need to see an effect on the world at large through one's initiatives dominate much of the person's life activity. The person experiences self most immediately through projecting dreams into the world and seeing them manifested as reality. Planets in the fire houses affect the individual's ATTITUDE TOWARD LIFE ITSELF and the person's entire sense of faith and confidence in self. The keyword that sums up the essential meaning of the fire houses is **IDENTITY**; for our sense of identity, our sense of *being*, determines our attitude toward life in general.

AIR HOUSES ("THE TRINITY OF RELATIONSHIP"—3, 7, 11): These houses are associated not only with social contacts and relationships of all types, but also with CONCEPTS. The person with an emphasis on these houses lives in the mind and in relationships. Concepts and the sharing of those concepts dominate much of the person's life activity. The person experiences self most immediately through a sense of mutual understanding with others and through discovering and expressing the reality and importance of specific ideas or theories. Planets in the air houses affect the individual's interests, associations, mode of verbal expression, and social life. The keywords for the air houses are **SOCIAL** and **INTELLECTUAL**.

The following presents a concise formulation of the keywords described above:

Mode of Expression	*Level of Experience*
Angular: *Action*	Water: *Soul & Emotional*
Succedent: *Security*	Earth: *Material*
Cadent: *Learning*	Fire: *Identity*
	Air: *Social & Intellectual*

The Water Houses

The Fourth House

The fourth house is the area of direct **ACTION** on the **EMOTIONAL** and **SOUL** level. All action at this level of experience is necessarily conditioned by factors beyond our control. Traditionally the fourth house is related to, among other things, the home and family. In what area of life do we act so much on the basis of habit and emotion as when dealing with our family members? This house also symbolizes the home as a source of renewal and nurturing (or the lack of it).

Those who have a strong emphasis on the fourth house have a need to act at the deepest emotional level in order to assimilate the essence of their experience in childhood and youth. They yearn for *peace for the individual self* and therefore almost always have a strong need for privacy. There is often a focus on activities that develop the inner life and encourage soul development.

The Eighth House

The eighth house represents the need to find **EMOTIONAL SECURITY** and **SOUL SECURITY**. The sexuality associated with this house is prompted not merely by instinct, but also by a need to experience ultimate emotional security through merging with another person. Many people also attempt to gain this feeling of security by achieving power and influence over other people or through financial dealings.

Although people with eighth house emphasis may seek security in material values, power, sex, or psychic knowledge, a real feeling of emotional and soul security can only exist when the tumultuous emotional conflicts always symbolized by this house begin to subside. The occult studies associated with this house are primarily useful as a means of attaining inner peace through knowledge of the deepest laws of life. The sexuality of the eighth house is an expression of the urge to be reborn through union with a greater power than the isolated self. In short, this house symbolizes the desire for a *state of emotional peace* which can be arrived at only by growing free from desires and compulsive willfulness.

This house is also concerned with issues and activities associated with energy released from various forms and the energy underlying form: thus, healing, occult studies, sex, transformative methods, and investments and financial obligations.

The Twelfth House

The twelfth house is the area of **LEARNING** on the **EMOTIONAL** and **SOUL** level. This learning takes place through the gradual growth of awareness that accompanies loneliness and deep suffering, through selfless service, or through devotion to a higher ideal. At the deepest level, this house indicates the urge to seek *peace for the soul* through surrender to a higher unity, through devotion to a transcendent ideal, and through freedom from the ghosts of past thoughts and actions.

The Earth Houses

The Tenth House

This earth house deals with **ACTION** on the **MATERIAL** level; and, traditionally, it is said to represent one's position in the world, reputation, ambition, and vocation. The action that anyone performs in the material world is the basis upon which his reputation rests. And, in order to act effectively in the material world, one needs the *authority* to do so—another meaning of the tenth house. The keywords also clarify the tenth house's traditional association with the specific ambition that one hopes to accomplish in the world or feels *called* to contribute to society, the latter case being a sense of destiny beyond personal ambition.

The Second House

The second house's keywords are **MATERIAL SECURITY.** These words aptly describe the relationship of this house to money, earnings, possessions, and the desire to control things and people. The keywords also clarify a broader principle underlying such inclinations, for many people with a strong second-house emphasis are concerned not with money itself as much as they are hungry for security in the material world. To ensure this security, they require an abundance of resources, often including money. Attitudes toward all these things are usually clearly symbolized by second house factors.

Another source of *material security* often seen in those with an emphasized second house is the importance of the relaxing, stabilizing influence that the *experience of nature* gives them. For many, an innate and meaningful attunement to the natural environment is a source of security of equal importance to material possessions. Along the same lines, one can say that the attachment to form and to things is an expression of a strong relationship to the earth.

The Sixth House

The sixth house has been associated with work, health, service, duties, and helpfulness. When we see that the underlying principle of the sixth house is that of **LEARNING** through immediate experience with **MATERIAL** affairs, we can easily understand the motivation behind these activities. We learn about our material body's needs and limitations chiefly through health problems, and gain practical insight into ourselves through everyday performance of our work and duties. All these areas of experience help us to learn humility, to accept our limitations, and to take responsibility for our own state of health, both physical and psychological. When it is understood that the sixth house represents a phase of purification, refinement, and developing humility through immediate contact with the material level of experience, we can begin to interpret this house in a true and positive way.

The Fire Houses

The First House

The angular fire house is the first house and represents one's **IDENTITY** in **ACTION.** Traditionally, this house is associated with the energy and appearance of the physical body. Using the keywords, one can see that the body *is* one's identity in action. People recognize us and are influenced by our most characteristic manner of physical movement and expression. The keywords also point toward the forms of creativity, initiative, leadership, and self-expression that are *uniquely* ours and shown by first house factors.

The Fifth House

The succedent fire house, the fifth, represents the search for **IDENTITY SECURITY.** Those with an emphasis on this house are seeking a secure sense of self by identifying with things or people in which they see themselves reflected: things we have made, things and people we love, being appreciated, noticed, or acclaimed by others. An urge toward *significance* and the attempt to gain a secure sense of identity are reflected in each matter commonly associated with this house: children, creativity, and love affairs.

This house is also associated with risk-taking. Virtually all fifth house matters (gambling, love affairs, having children, creativity, and publicly expressing oneself) are essentially risky. We can learn from this that we become more secure in our identity by developing the ability to take risks. A rigid, static sense of identity is not secure.

The Ninth House

The cadent fire house, the ninth, represents **LEARNING** on the level of **IDENTITY**; in other words, *learning who one really is.* From this essential principle flow all the religious and philosophical attitudes, travels, searchings, and activities with which this house is usually associated. People with an emphasis on this house are drawn to activities which widen their horizons of self-awareness, enlarge the scope of their understanding, and help them to gain a perspective on human nature and the broadest possible overview of the universe. Those with a strong ninth house need a sense of personal development and a feeling of space and vast possibilities.

The Air Houses

The Seventh House

The seventh house symbolizes **ACTION** at the **SOCIAL** and **INTELLECTUAL** level. One-to-one relationship is the basic experience of this house; and all social structures and activities depend on the quality of personal relationship. On the individual level, the quality of a person's chief partnership has such impact that its influence pervades all the other areas of life: health, finance, sex, children, professional success, etc.; and therefore such partnerships have a powerful impact on one's social life and intellectual development.

The Eleventh House

The succedent air house is the eleventh and represents the search for **SOCIAL** and **INTELLECTUAL SECURITY**. Those whose natal charts focus on the eleventh house tend to join groups or align themselves with friends who share their intellectual bent, although they may not agree at all on specifics. Their search for intellectual security also leads them into vast systems of thought, whether political, metaphysical, or scientific. The most effective way that a person with a strong eleventh house can achieve the security he or she seeks is to establish a strong sense of individual *purpose* which not only fulfills his personal needs but also *harmonizes with the needs of society as a whole*.

The Third House

The third house is the field of **LEARNING** at the **SOCIAL** and **INTELLECTUAL** level. It therefore represents all forms of exchange of information, such as basic communication skills, media work, merchandising, etc. Those with a strong third house emphasis have a deep, sometimes insatiable need to communicate with others and often an ability to deal in an easy and friendly way with people of the most diverse qualities and interests (depending on which planets are in this house). Whereas the learning of the ninth house comes about through the use of the inspired intuitive mind, the learning of the third house occurs through the application of one's own logic, reason, and endless curiosity.

This house represents not only all issues of communication with others, but also how the person's mind functions. Planets in this house reveal how we use our mind and communicate our thoughts and also how our thinking patterns have an impact on our life in general.

Interpretive Guidelines for Understanding House Placements

I have found the following four guidelines to be extraordinarily reliable in understanding birth charts and the individuals' lives reflected in these charts:*

a) The houses show where one's attention is drawn. The more planets in a house, the more attention must be paid to that field of experience in one's life.

b) The houses show where one most naturally focuses one's energies. One expresses the energy of a planet in the activities and experiences related to the house in which it is located.

> EXAMPLE: Venus in the 4th house. One most naturally expresses the emotional and love energy of Venus in private surroundings and in experiences related to domestic, family, or parental matters. The urge for pleasure and social comfort is most easily expressed in one's private life and in one's own home.

---

*IMPORTANT NOTE: The reader will notice in the next few pages that the guidelines for interpreting houses are not as specific as the Interpretive Guidelines for Planets in Signs, and there are good reasons for that. First of all, I much prefer an open-ended approach to understanding the houses in any particular chart, since each house has virtually an infinite number of derivative meanings and since each individual's circumstances, values, background, and level of consciousness comprise a completely unique pattern. Secondly, it is easier and more appropriate to be quite specific about planets in signs since the signs reveal the real energy at work in life and the houses are quite secondary. For example, one can do a great deal of accurate work in astrology using no houses whatsoever, as one must do when there is no accurate birth time available. Even then, one can do approximately 60 to 90% of the practically useful astrology possible with that person. And finally, the sign position and aspects to a planet are so important and dominant that trying to interpret a planet's house position in isolation, without reference to sign position and aspects, often results in highly inaccurate assessments. It is far preferable to use reliable guidelines and discover the reality in a dialogue.

c) The house placement of a planet shows where one *most immediately confronts* the dimension of experience symbolized by that planet.

> EXAMPLE: Venus in the 4th house. One most immediately confronts the experience of love and emotional sharing through private activities, establishing a family, or pursuing soul development.

d) The house placement of a planet shows where one naturally seeks to fulfill the needs symbolized by that planet.

> EXAMPLE: Mercury in the 7th house. One seeks to fulfill one's intellectual and communication needs through close relationships and in various partnerships.

Interpretive Guidelines for Each Planet's House Position

Using the following guidelines in a one-to-one in-person *dialogue* (rather than in a traditional one-sided astrological "reading") will enable both people to experience a surprising joint session of discovery.

Whatever house the **SUN** is in, it is there that one most immediately experiences one's essential self and creative essence. This field of experience vitalizes the person and is essential to one's sense of well-being.

Whatever house the **MOON** is in, it is there that one looks for emotional fulfillment, emotional security, and a sense of comfort. In this field of experience, one will most immediately experience a sense of belonging and a more stable and clear self-image.

Whatever house **MERCURY** is in, it is there that one most immediately experiences the meaning of real communication; in this field of experience, the intellect is constantly active. One may need a regular exchange of mental energy with other people in order to achieve clarity in this area of life.

Whatever house **VENUS** is in, it is there that one looks for pleasure, contentment, and happiness. It is in this field of experience that one can share one's self and one's affectionate feelings, and can develop a deeper sense of appreciation for others, as well as a feeling of being appreciated by others.

Whatever house **MARS** is in, it is there that one can tune in most immediately to one's assertiveness, courage, and capacity for initiative. It is this field of experience that is crucial to maintaining one's physical energy and health; ideally, activities in this area of life give one energy and stimulate one to rekindle the motivation to strive.

Whatever house **JUPITER** is in, it is there that one can most immediately experience faith, trust, and hope for the future. In this field of experience one can most easily develop an optimistic awareness of one's capacity for growth and self-improvement.

Whatever house **SATURN** is in, it is there that one can experience stability, structure, deep satisfaction, and meaning in life. In this area of life, one must work and take on responsibility, and accept pressure as a necessary molding of one's character. This house invariably represents a field of experience that is especially important to the person.

Whatever house **URANUS** is in, it is there that one can most immediately experience one's uniqueness, originality, genius, objectivity, and need for excitement. In this area of life, one expresses oneself freely and intuitively, inventively and experimentally. Also, in this house one can tune into issues that concern society at large and contribute to positive changes in the world.

Whatever house **NEPTUNE** is in, it is there that one can experience most directly the reality of the non-material, the mystical, the transcendent, and the inspiring. It is there that one can most readily tap into a stream of imagination, as well as where one will habitually try to escape from routine, oppressive, uninspiring conditions. This house can in some cases give you a clue to what type of experiences can help you to spiritualize and refine your life. It is also the house where one may idealize things excessively.

Whatever house **PLUTO** is in, it is there that one experiences a thorough transformation in one's attitudes and in the expression of what had been deeply compulsive habit patterns. One usually has a particularly deep and thorough approach in this field of experience, and confronting this area of life honestly and bluntly can contribute toward the evolution of one's consciousness.

A Crucial Point for Interpreting Houses

One should note that planets that are conjunct a house cusp within 6°, *on either side of the cusp*, should be regarded as strongly <u>in</u> that particular house. For example, if one's 5th house cusp is 24° Sagittarius and one has Venus at 18° of Sagittarius, Venus is *conjunct* the 5th cusp. Although most traditional astrologers would interpret that placement *exclusively* as a 4th house Venus, this old approach assumes that houses are discrete little boxes of life activity that abruptly start and finish. However, experience teaches that the houses are fields of experience— like fields of energy—that slowly develop, peak, and then drop off in strength.*

Perhaps the most important application of this interpretive guideline is the proper understanding of conjunctions to the horizon line of the chart—that is, when a planet is conjunct either the Ascendant or Descendant. I cannot count the number of times I have heard people say, often in a confused tone of voice, things like: "I have a 12th house Mars, but it acts like a first house planet"; or, "I don't have anything in the 7th house, although Saturn is in the 6th only 4° from the 7th cusp, and a 7th house Saturn would make sense if you look at my life." One might say here that, if it walks like a duck and quacks like a duck, it probably is a duck. These people do have a first house Mars and a 7th house Saturn!

Any planet which conjuncts the Ascendant or Descendant within 6° should be considered a first or a seventh house planet. That planet therefore represents a dimension of experience that is profoundly important, and sometimes even dominant, in the individual's entire outlook on life. Likewise, any planet conjunct the Midheaven (also called the MC, which is the tenth house

---

*The findings in Michel Gauquelin's research would tend to confirm the importance of conjunctions to house cusps, even if the planet is on the preceding house side of the cusp.

cusp in most house systems) or its opposite point, the IC, also has an important impact on motivation, reputation, security, parental influence, and so on—all of the tenth and fourth house matters. This will be true even if the planet is apparently in the third or ninth house, so long as it is within 6° of the MC or IC.

Interpretive Guidelines for the Signs on the House Cusps

The signs on the succedent and cadent house cusps are parts of an interrelated system that can provide insight in much the same way that the signs on the four angular house cusps (1, 4, 7, 10) can. However, the signs on the non-angular cusps are not as prominent or noticeable in the personality (unless they contain planets), and should not be over-emphasized in interpretation. In general, one can rely on the following guidelines for practical chart interpretation, always keeping in mind that a house cusp near the beginning or end of a sign may in fact fall in a different sign if a different house system is used or if the birth time is even a few minutes from accurate! This is yet another reason to be cautious and moderate in using the signs on the cusps in interpretation. In general, it is best to focus on the houses where planets are located, rather than attributing too much importance to empty houses or signs on cusps as isolated interpretive factors.

a) The sign on a cusp shows the *approach to* and *attitude toward* the field of experience symbolized by that house.

> EXAMPLES: Libra on the 6th house cusp. One approaches in a balanced way the process of learning through experience in all material affairs. The person with Libra on the 6th cusp quickly senses and attempts to harmonize any discord in the work situation or in one's own health.
>
> Taurus on the 11th house cusp. One approaches the search for social and intellectual security by maintaining steadiness and a firm grip on reality. One feels more intellectually secure through the knowledge that a physical, tangible reality does exist. Socially, one seeks security through steadfast loyalty shared with others.

b) The sign on a cusp shows the *qualities of experience* related to that house's field of experience and the specific energies activated by that scope of activity.

> EXAMPLE: Pisces on the 2nd house cusp. One's experience with material security often can take on an elusive or confusing quality. No matter how practical the person may be otherwise, the experience of having secure material resources always contains some element of idealism or doubt. Seemingly, the person is learning to let go of a sense of control in this area.

CHAPTER 8

UNDERSTANDING PLANETARY ASPECTS

The dynamic interactions between the various energies of life are represented on an individual level by the "aspects" in a natal chart—that is, the angles between planets and between the Ascendant or Midheaven and the planets. Aspects have been spoken of as "lines of force" between the various energy centers (planets) in the energy field mapped by the chart. In the birth chart, which reveals this energy field with remarkable precision, the aspects are measured within the 360° circle. This book will concentrate on the most commonly used aspects—the ones occurring every 30°, all of which I consider "major aspects" that are reliable and illuminating. The mathematical theory of aspects has been explained in many other books,* and we will not dwell upon it here. This chapter is meant to give guidelines for the practical understanding of aspects in chart interpretation.

---

*See especially Chapter 6 of the author's *Astrology, Karma & Transformation*. That chapter also includes quite detailed explanations of many specific aspects.

Aspects can be categorized in two groups:

DYNAMIC or **CHALLENGING** aspects: This refers to the square (90°), opposition (180°), quincunx (150°), and sometimes, depending upon the harmony of the planets and signs involved, the conjunction (0°) and the semi-sextile (30°)* These angles correspond with the experience of inner tension and usually prompt some sort of definite action or at least the development of greater awareness in the areas indicated. Although the term "inharmonious" (as well as "difficult" or "bad") is often applied to these aspects by astrological writers, these terms can be misleading, since it is possible for the individual to develop a relatively harmonious mode of expression for these energies by taking on responsibilities, work, or other challenges which are capable of absorbing the full intensity of the energy being released. The challenging aspects show that the energies involved (and thus the life-dimensions of the individual whose chart has such an aspect) do not vibrate in harmony. They tend to interfere with each other's expression and to create stress within the energy field, as if two energy waves were in a discordant relationship to each other, setting up what one might call an unstable or irritating tone. This irritation or instability can, however, lead the individual to take steps toward resolving the tension. For example, a dynamic aspect between Mercury and Mars can manifest as an impatience (Mars) to communicate (Mercury), a strong drive (Mars) to learn (Mercury), the tendency to assert too forcefully (Mars) one's ideas and opinions (Mercury), an irritable nervous system, an overly critical nature, etc. If the irritability and inner tension are successfully controlled and directed, however, such an individual may well be able to focus the tremendous drive toward learning into the development of exceptional skills which

---

*I would not urge beginning students of astrology to use the 45° and 135° aspects, although they are quite commonly used by astrologers. I personally have not found them particularly useful. Approximately 50% of these aspects will involve planets in harmonious elements and thus be considered mildly harmonious or flowing aspects. The other 50% involve planets in inharmonious elements and would therefore be considered moderately dynamic or challenging aspects.

require keen intelligence. Such a planetary relationship may be expressed as follows:*

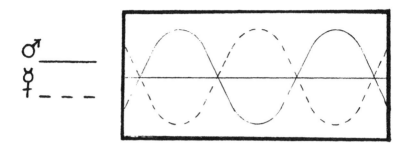

HARMONIOUS or **FLOWING** aspects: This refers to the trine (120°), sextile (60°), and some of the conjunctions (0°) (depending on the planets involved) and semi-sextiles (30°) (depending on the harmony of the planets and the elements of the signs involved). These angles correspond with spontaneous abilities, talents, and modes of understanding and expression which the individual is able to utilize and develop with relative ease and consistency. These abilities constitute a set of steady and reliable personal assets upon which the person may draw at any time. Although the individual may prefer to concentrate his or her energy and attention on the more dynamic, challenging aspects of life, these flowing aspects do represent the *potential* for developing extraordinary talents. But in contrast with the dynamic aspects, they are most indicative of a *state of being* and an innate and *spontaneous attunement* to an established and comfortable channel of expression; whereas the dynamic aspects indicate the need for *adjustment* through effort, direct action, and the development of new channels of self-expression. The harmonious aspects show that the energies involved (and thus the two dimensions of the individual's being) vibrate in harmony and thus *reinforce* each other within the person's energy field, similar to two waves harmonizing and blending into a unified

---

*For a more detailed explanation of the following two graphs and the energy flow they represent, see pages 110 and 111 of *Astrology, Karma & Transformation*.

expression of complex energies. To use again the example of Mercury and Mars, a harmonious aspect between them indicates an automatic blending of the two energies which can produce mental strength, the power to assert one's ideas, a strong nervous system, and the ability to project one's ideas into definite action. It is as if Mercury lends its intelligence to guide the Mars self-assertion, while simultaneously Mars energizes the Mercurian perception and verbal expression. Such a planetary relationship might be visually expressed like this:

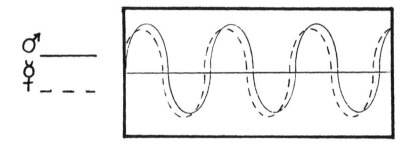

An important point is that *each aspect must be evaluated according to the nature of the planets and signs involved.* There is considerable evidence that some of the trine aspects correspond with wasteful or problematic conditions in many cases, despite the traditional teaching that these are "beneficial" aspects. For example, Uranus trines are common in the charts of people who are particularly self-centered, unable to cooperate, given to the "I know it all" syndrome, and so speeded up with excitement about their own interests that they are extremely impatient with others. By contrast, the dynamic aspects are often found to symbolize energy that can be expressed with great concentration, power, and creativity, although they do often also show conflicts and problems (sometimes simultaneously). If we can begin to see that there is value inherent in challenge and effort and even in pain, we can begin to understand the aspects in an accurate, deep, and practical way.

A Law for Interpreting Aspects

My favorite law for interpreting aspects is:

The planets in the signs represent the basic *urges toward expression* and *needs for fulfillment,* but the aspects reveal the actual state of the energy flow and thus how much personal *effort* is needed in order to express a particular urge or to fulfill a particular need.

In other words, a particular aspect does not tell us if a person will experience or achieve something specific; but it does tell us how much effort will be required, in a relative sense, to achieve a given result. This is an interpretive guideline that is worth studying in depth and remembering. It is absolutely crucial to understand this law if one is going to interpret aspects accurately and subtly.

The Major Aspects

Here are some guidelines for the interpretation of the major aspects:*

CONJUNCTION (0°): Any conjunction in an individual chart should be regarded as important, since it indicates an intense merging and interaction of two life energies. The most powerful of all conjunctions are those involving one of the "personal planets" (Sun, Moon, Mercury, Venus, and Mars) or the Ascendant. Such conjunctions always characterize particularly strong modes of energy flow and personal expression (by planet and sign) and dominant emphases in the person's life (by house). The keynote of the conjunction is *action* and *self-projection*.

SEMI-SEXTILE (30°): This is traditionally considered a minor aspect, but at times it can be more noticeable even than the conjunction, depending upon the planets involved and the other aspects to the two planets. Planets in semi-sextile are constantly interacting and building on the energy of each other. They do not usually generate the stress of a square and are in fact usually gentler in effect than the quincunx, but they are persistent and almost always in evidence if the aspect is quite close.

SEXTILE (60°): The sextile seems to be an aspect of openness to the new: new people, new ideas, new attitudes; and it symbolizes the potential for making new connections with either people or ideas that can ultimately lead to new learning. This aspect usually involves signs of harmonious elements, and thus compatible energies. The sextile shows an area of life where one can cultivate not only a new level of understanding but also a greater degree of objectivity which can lead to a feeling of great freedom. It indicates an automatic, natural attunement and sometimes a definite skill.

---

*I consider *all* multiples of 30° to be "major" aspects, in contrast to most astrological textbooks, which treat the semi-sextile and quincunx as minor aspects. In many people, a semi-sextile or quincunx may be more obvious or active than a trine.

SQUARE (90°): The square usually involves planets in inharmonious elements and thus calls forth significant effort in order to integrate such divergent energies. Any close square involving one of the personal planets represents a major life challenge. A square aspect shows where energy must be *released*, usually through action of a definite sort, in order that a new structure may be built. Many astrologers have written that the square aspect has the nature of Saturn: it represents what you *have* to deal with. Another Saturnian feature related to the square is *fear*, for we are often afraid of dealing with whatever is symbolized by the squares in our charts. Fearing challenge restricts the energy available to deal effectively with whatever problem is at hand.

TRINE (120°): A trine aspect represents an easy flow of energy into established channels of expression. One does not need to build a new structure or to make marked adjustments in one's life in order to utilize this energy creatively. The planets involved in the trine reveal dimensions of life and specific energies which are naturally integrated and which flow together harmoniously. (Note that trines are commonly between signs of the same element, which is the basis for the harmony of energies.) Such an aspect often shows a way of *being*, however, rather than a way of *doing*; one often takes for granted the abilities and talents shown by the trine and thus sometimes does not feel challenged to make the effort required to use the energy constructively.

QUINCUNX (or INCONJUNCT) (150°): This aspect indicates a strong flow of energy between those dimensions of life symbolized by the planets involved, but the individual may feel that the experience of those energies is too compulsive or consistently annoying. It is difficult to remain aware of both energies simultaneously, and one usually has to make a conscious, concerted effort to do so. Note that the quincunx aspect usually involves signs that are not only of inharmonious elements but also of different modalities. (E.g., a quincunx between planets in Gemini and Capricorn involves mutable Air and cardinal Earth— quite a dissimilarity but potentially a combination of deep understanding and practical skill.) It is important to be aware of both energies, because it often seems that the expression of each of the two factors involved is dependent upon the other. Thus, if one is not conscious of both energies, one of them may interfere with the other, causing a problem because the energies are not well integrated. Dealing with this aspect effectively requires discrimination in subtly adjusting one's approach to those areas of life rather than trying to force a solution.

OPPOSITION (180°): The opposition, particularly since it usually involves planets in harmonious elements, indicates a degree of *over-stimulation* in the person's energy field which often manifests as a feeling of being caught in the middle of completely opposite tendencies. This is usually felt most directly as a constant challenge in the area of personal relationships. There is often a marked lack of objectivity since the individual tends to engage in "projection" of different sides of his or her nature onto others; and thus there is some difficulty in distinguishing what is yours and what is somebody else's. Having an opposition in one's chart is similar to being stretched between two contrasting, sometimes contradictory tendencies. Opposite signs are similar in many ways and in fact complementary, but there is no denying that they are also totally opposed in many ways.

Orbs & Planetary Interactions

The aspects, of course, do not consist solely of mathematical angles. The planets and signs involved in an aspect describe the energies that are interacting within a person. Planets involved in *close* aspects represent dimensions of experience that are rarely expressed or felt in isolation. They always affect each other, no matter which specific major aspect they are making in the natal chart. In many respects, the *type* of aspect between two or more planets is less significant in interpretation than is the fact that those two specific energies are constantly interacting.

In other words, for example, the Sun closely aspecting Uranus will have most of the same qualities whether the aspect is a square, trine, quincunx, or semi-sextile. There is certainly considerable difference among the aspects, as described in the previous section; however, I tend to concentrate most upon the interactions and blendings of the specific planetary energies involved in an aspect. The negative and the positive manifestations of a certain planetary combination can co-exist and both be expressed in a particular individual, no matter what exact angle separates the two planets. The exactitude of the aspect is invariably important in relation to the level of intensity that a particular aspect manifests.

In fact, over the years I have been convinced that the most exact aspects are always the most powerful and should be given the most attention in chart interpretation. Beginning and intermediate students of astrology would be well advised to look to the closest aspect or aspects in any chart being considered, early in the consultation or chart evaluation. Many astrological books have advised students to allow orbs* as large as 12° when interpreting aspects. My experience leads me to conclude that: *The more one knows what works effectively in astrology, the tighter one's orbs get.*

---

*An "orb" in astrological tradition is the number of degrees from exactitude that is allowed while still considering the dynamic influence of that aspect to be in effect.

I would have to state that an orb of 8° or 9° for most aspects is completely unacceptable because that aspect is not signifi-cantly in effect! That is to say, those energies are not interacting with any degree of dynamism. Only in the case of Sun, Moon, or Ascendant aspects would I ever consider allowing an orb of over 7°, and an orb of even 6° is getting very wide for the other aspects. I would strongly urge beginning students to focus on aspects which have orbs of no more than 5° in the early stages of their studies.

The evaluation of any specific aspect in a birth chart also has to take into consideration not only the intrinsic nature of the planets involved, but also whether each planet is in a "con-genial" sign—that is, a sign through which it can freely express its essential nature. If the sign position of a planet alone represents a built-in conflict, even a harmonious aspect might manifest less harmoniously. Whereas, if the sign position of a planet is especially comfortable and compatible, even a close challenging aspect may not represent so severe a test as it might at first appear.

In summary, each specific aspect in any chart is actually com-pletely unique, since it is woven into the entire chart structure (and thus into the fabric of one's life) in an intricate way. Hence, one must learn the basic principles of aspect interpretation to do accurate work, but ultimately it takes broad experience to be able to understand the intricacies of these essential interpretive factors in actual charts of individuals.

Guidelines to Planetary
Interchanges & Blendings

It is important to note that aspects between the three outer planets, in themselves and when isolated from other primary factors in the chart, should not be considered a major factor in interpretation. Uranus, Neptune, and Pluto carry a transpersonal meaning and clarify some aspects of mass psychology for an entire generation, as they remain in one sign for many years. All too often, new students of astrology become very upset about, for example, a square between Uranus and Neptune, only to find out after more experience that *everyone* born during a period of a couple of years had that same aspect in their natal charts! This is one more instance of the need for beginners in astrology to focus on the essentials and to learn to discriminate right from the start between the primary and the innumerable secondary features in any chart.

However, should a person have, for example, Neptune conjunct Saturn, both of which form a square aspect (or 90° angle) to the Sun, that *entire configuration*—blending the Sun, Saturn, and Neptune energies—would then have to receive considerable attention.

In this book, in order to remain focused on the primary, reliable features of the chart, I am providing guidelines only for aspects that are absolutely *essential* and invariably important for everyone—that is, only those involving the five personal planets, Jupiter, Saturn, and the Ascendant. As just mentioned, the other aspects are relatively unimportant on an individual level, except insofar as they tie in with the major placements, structures, and themes of the chart.*

---

*Even aspects involving Jupiter or Saturn and one of the outer three planets should not be given particularly great emphasis if the aspect is isolated from the major factors in the chart. If, however, a sign ruled by Jupiter or Saturn is strongly emphasized in the chart, then all aspects to Jupiter or Saturn gain in importance.

This section provides brief guidelines for the interpretation of aspects, based upon the planetary principles involved. Blending these energies in an accurate way will develop over time with further experience. It should also be emphasized that a deep understanding will develop much more quickly from in-person dialogues than from mere book-learning or speculative "readings" done for people one has never seen. As in other sections of this book, the key phrases included here are meant to encourage understanding of the basics and to provoke independent thought in applying the principles involved to people's real situations. This is one reason (along with the tendency to judge aspects too rigidly as "good" or "bad") why the planetary interchanges (or "blendings" of their energies) that follow do not generally distinguish between the challenging and the harmonious aspects. The most important thing is to understand how any particular pair of planets works together, and there is no denying that the negative manifestations of a particular interchange are often seen in those who have those planets in a harmonious aspect. Likewise, there is no denying that many people who have two planets in challenging aspect express many of the positive qualities that rigid traditional notions would lead one to believe were only found when the planets were in harmonious or flowing relationship with each other.

Here and there in the following guidelines I do mention some often-observed differences between the harmonious and challenging interchanges of a particular pair of planets, but I do this mainly when I have come to feel that they are usually reliable comparisons. I have also included now and then some especially useful comments that help summarize the general meaning of a certain type of aspect or certain groups of aspects. Many of these comments I found extremely useful when teaching astro'-ogy. I should also acknowledge how helpful the lectures of Frances Sakoian were in my learning to differentiate between all the different types of aspects. Those talks were given approximately 20 years ago, and yet I still find so many of my notes and notebooks referring to things she said that some of the phrases in the following sections are probably almost direct quotes from her talks. My own observations and notes are by now so interwoven with quotes from her and other astrologers that it is impossible to give specific references and appropriate credit for all the various ideas learned from others.

Aspects with the Sun

The aspects with the Sun have a strong impact on the physical vitality, the ease of self-expression, what spurs one on to creativity, what you identify with, and how easily the ego attains satisfaction. Any planet in conjunction with the Sun symbolizes something essential about the person's entire identity. In general, planets in harmonious relationship to the Sun encourage a sense of well-being, whereas the challenging aspects with the Sun reveal an obstacle to attaining that sense of well-being which must be overcome or adjusted to.

Sun-Moon Interchanges

⊙
☽
Creative energy interacts with the urge for emotional security; the need to creatively express one's individuality comfortably and confidently

How one's self-image blends with one's vitality and need for self-expression

[All Sun-Moon aspects are extraordinarily important. They have a tremendous impact on one's sense of self and one's health and confidence. The harmonious interchanges show that your feelings reinforce the expression of your best self and your most central purpose and aims. The more challenging aspects often show that the instinctive feelings and sense of self inhibit the free expression of the creative self; with the square and opposition especially, it is often hard to feel good about oneself and an inner tension in the core personality seems a permanent feature of the psyche.]

Sun-Mercury Interchanges (Only the conjunction and semi-sextile are possible.*)

⊙
☿
Communication is vital, lively, and radiant—sometimes no perspective on one's own thoughts

---

*It should be mentioned here that I have found the old idea of a planet being "combust" (i.e., devastated when conjunct the Sun) to be completely invalid. Very often those with Mercury conjunct the Sun, for example, are extremely intelligent.

The need to establish connections with others unites with creative energy—often an instinctive intelligence with a creative flair

Sun-Venus Interchanges (Only the conjunction, semi-sextile, and semi-square are possible.)

Urge for pleasure merges with the urge to be and to create—often artistic

Sense of individuality is heightened when exchanging energy with others—often a marked kindness or sweetness

Sun-Mars Interchanges

Vital creative energy is inflamed by feelings of desire, and desires are constantly energized by the power of the entire identity

Physical energy blends with the essential self, producing an intense dynamism and need for action

[All Sun-Mars aspects tend to give a great boost to the vital force and reveal an aggressive urge to express oneself and to prove oneself. Considerable ego gratification is desired, and the person is therefore sometimes arrogant. Leadership is likely, as well as the courageous desire to pioneer into new areas of achievement and creative action.]

Sun-Jupiter Interchanges

The need to be recognized interacts with the urge to expand beyond the self, to become one with something bigger than self

Sense of individuality incorporates faith and openness to grace

[All Sun-Jupiter aspects show a great need for ego-gratification by doing something big, something that will make others take notice. A very common blending in those involved with stage work, big business, etc.]

Sun-Saturn Interchanges

☉ Urge to be and create combines with the need for stability;
ħ that conservative tendency often challenging the self-
confidence and sense of well-being

One's need for safety and security colors the tone of one's
essential being, making one appear older than one's peers,
even at an early age

[Saturn is often hard on the Sun, even when the aspect is
a trine or sextile. One feels keenly aware of one's limits and faults,
to the point in many cases of exaggerating them and even in-
dulging in too much self-condemnation or self-inhibition. The
expression of one's creativity (and love) can be blocked because
of defensiveness and feelings of inadequacy and unworthiness.
The one area where these people are not practical is in their
understanding of themselves and the scope of expression that
they need! Experience and time are the only solutions to these
aspects, for one can learn one's true worth through tangible
results and handling responsibility.]

Sun-Uranus Interchanges

☉ Radiant inner self blends with an urge toward change, ex-
♅ citement, experimentation, and rebellion; one's vitality
thrives on this freedom

One's sense of individuality incorporates originality and
inventiveness—often very creative and unconventional

[An unconventional quality pervades those who have any
aspect between these planets, and in fact an obstinate self-
centeredness is common to many. Although often interesting,
lively, stimulating people, they often feel that people misinter-
pret them or never understand them. This is usually true, partly
because the person is so completely unpredictable. They generally have the courage of their unusual convictions, and at best
they display a kind of crazy sincerity and honesty which elicits
bewilderment but also respect. Their dislike of monotony often
leads them to exhibit what Carl Payne Tobey called the "hobo

spirit,'' wanting change for the sake of change or tossing aside that which most would want to retain.]

Sun-Neptune Interchanges

The identity and basic consciousness incorporate the urge to transcend the material world through imagination, idealism, or spiritual pursuits

One's realization of the spiritual dimension of experience colors the mode of self-expression but can cause confusion in one's sense of identity

[Those with this blending desperately need honest feedback from others in order to achieve a realistic, clear sense of self. They tend either to overrate or underrate their abilities and personal worth.]

Sun-Pluto Interchanges

One's perception of life is infused with a powerful urge toward depth of experience and total rebirth

The inner self focuses one's willpower on reform and transformation—one's own or that of the outer world

[Invariably, those with a close aspect between Pluto and the Sun have far more depth of insight, personal seriousness, and awareness of the darker or harsher side of life than the rest of their chart might indicate. They also have a tremendous persistence and thoroughness that sometimes surprises others since it may not be at all obvious.]

Sun-Ascendant Interchanges

The challenge of how much of one's true self to express outwardly is a central issue of the whole life

Creative impulses and the need to express oneself freely stimulates action and exerts an influence that others cannot ignore

Aspects with the Moon

The aspects with the Moon show not only to what extent one has a positive and accurate self-image and an inner confidence and security, but also how one is able to express and make use of one's deeper feelings and creative imagination. Are one's immediate reactions to life's experiences useful and supportive, or inappropriate and confusing? What encourages, or interferes with, one's emotional tranquility is sharply revealed by the lunar aspects. The entire way one *reacts* and adjusts to the ebbs and flows of life is symbolized by the Moon and its aspects. Perhaps more than with any other planet, the more challenging aspects with the Moon do indeed tend to be rather predictable in their problematic outcome; and the harmonious lunar aspects tend to reliably indicate the more positive, pleasant, comfortable lunar manifestations.

This is not to say that one cannot adjust to having dynamic lunar aspects in one's chart; one can indeed work on objectivity. The challeging aspects show that one will have to *work*, however, to gain the sort of objectivity that comes naturally with harmonious lunar aspects. The Moon is in fact the key to *objectivity about oneself*. A harmoniously aspected Moon in a comfortable sign has a natural objectivity about the self and often therefore a fairly accurate self-image. But when the Moon is stressfully aspected, one tends to take everything personally, with no detachment about oneself. Hence, in that case one is not able to adjust easily to changing circumstances, and one's self-image is often quite inaccurate in the areas indicated by planets, signs, and houses involved.

Also, when the Moon is *conjunct* another planet, there is usually considerable lack of awareness and objectivity about that planet's dimension of experience. This is not to say that all conjunctions with the Moon are to be regarded as challenging aspects, but it does mean that whatever is indicated by the conjunction comes unconsciously and automatically. Sometimes it is indeed a blessing that helps one get through life. Who would not like to be born with Jupiter or Venus conjunct the Moon?

A guideline for understanding all the more dynamic lunar aspects is the following concept from Robert C. Jansky: The Moon in challenging aspects to Sun, Mercury, or Venus shows a feeling of being unable to express something that one feels. Whereas the Moon in challenging aspects to any of the other planets reveals a feeling of inadequacy for coping with life's demands.

Moon-Mercury Interchanges

☽ The emotions and the mind continually interact and stimulate fervently held opinions

☿ Rational understanding blends or clashes with a sense of emotional rightness and with one's subjective predisposition

Moon-Venus Interchanges

☽ Ability to give to and receive from others is helped or hindered by one's capacity to adapt spontaneously; one can be sensitive or over-sensitive to others

♀ Strong reactions to sensual pleasures and to all social interactions

Moon-Mars Interchanges

☽ Strong emotional reactions combine with drive and ambition to create an instinctive craving for action

♂ A restless need to achieve one's desires is dependent upon and strongly affects the need to feel right about self

Moon-Jupiter Interchanges

☽ Great sensitivity toward connection with a larger order, with going beyond the self—very tolerant of others' behavior but not always of their ideas

♃ A subconscious predisposition toward optimistic expansion and enthusiastic emotional reactions

[These aspects, although generally very "upbeat," buoyant, and generous, can expand the concern with self-image to the point of vanity and/or extreme self-consciousness. These people are sometimes overly concerned with the impression they make on others, and there is often a tendency to over-react emotionally and personally to minor things. Extravagance in dress, spending, and habits is common.]

Moon-Saturn Interchanges

☽ Domestic urge combines with the need for security through tangible achievement and handling responsibility

♄ The need always to exert a disciplined effort in order to feel right about self, often resulting in restrained emotional expression

[A tendency toward defensiveness and lack of self-confidence is very often a marked characteristic of these people. Even when they are not being criticized, they often think they are and thus are not open to hearing positive feedback about themselves. The childhood environment, especially in the case of the challenging aspects, was often oppressive, lonely, or otherwise burdensome.]

Moon-Uranus Interchanges

☽ One's reactions are always tinged with a streak of originality and unpredictability

♅ The need for unrestrained self-expression furthers or interferes with attaining inner support, security, and tranquility

[These aspects manifest in some very unusual, and sometimes dramatic, ways. There is a gnawing desire to change over one's identity in a radical way, and to rid oneself of all past encumbrances and conditioning. The urge to leave the past behind can be so strong that one changes one's name, symbolizing the desire to leave behind the old self-image. These people usually find it hard to be happy in the present since they are always powerfully aware of the impact of the past (the Moon) and the future (Uranus). The restlessness is often profound, since they are generally comfortable only when experiencing intense excitement; but that can of course wear out the body and the mind!]

Moon-Neptune Interchanges

☽ An urge to escape the limitations of the physical world pervades one's emotional responses; there can be great devotion to an ideal

♆ Self-image blends with the attempt to realize the spiritual dimension of experience and is secure only when the ideals come into focus

Moon-Pluto Interchanges

☽ Profound and deep responses; emotional security is related to a complete transformation and rebirth within oneself

♇ Inner contentment comes with acceptance of the need to focus one's emotions and willpower on remolding one's reaction patterns and eliminating old feelings and images

[A very interesting study could be based on these aspects, especially the challenging ones, with regard to the person's attitudes and emotions about parents and parenting. I have seen numerous people who have Moon conjunct or opposite Pluto who have a compulsion to mother people, but yet feel turmoil about it and often a deep fear of parenthood. In some cases, there has been a complete rejection of parenthood as an option (in both men and women), even when the person was comfortably married. There is sometimes a compulsive need for security but also a profound fear of dependency and loss. Sometimes there is a feeling of rejection by a parent (usually the mother) very early in life.]

Moon-Ascendant Interchanges

Perceptive intuitions color the approach to life, and a great sensitivity to the environment affects the moods strongly

The mode of self-expression in the outer world is affected by emotional and security urges, and the subconscious predispositions need to be expressed outwardly

Aspects with Mercury

The aspects with Mercury are a good indicator, not so much of the person's level of intelligence (as some astrologers and astrology books would have us believe), but rather of the person's ability to express and communicate. There are, after all, some very intelligent quiet people who may not have a particularly energized Mercury. Aspects with Mercury show how the conscious mind is attuned and how one expresses and communicates the flow of thought. Mercury is also important as a significator of the ability to *coordinate* all mental and physical functions, and it is known to correspond to the nervous system in general. A study of many professional athletes has shown me that powerful Mercury aspects (especially conjunctions) are very common, and yet these people are by no means intellectuals! But their mind/body coordination is exceptional.

Mercury-Venus Interchanges

☿ Urge to express one's intelligence is heightened by one's ability to share with and understand others
♀

♀ Tries to feel close to another through good communication and pleasant interchanges—a harmonious intellect striving for balance

Mercury-Mars Interchanges

☿ Conscious mind blends with physical energy (possibly good hand-eye coordination), stimulating both powerfully—an energized intellect
♂

♂ The need to act decisively helps focus the learning process and all communication

Mercury-Jupiter Interchanges

☿ The mode of communication and the way of thinking are deeply colored by a sense of breadth, expansion, and optimism—a wide-ranging, philosophical intellect, with overflowing curiosity
♃

Needs to explore broad interests and establish connections with others based on trust, a common faith in the future, and philosophical agreement

Mercury-Saturn Interchanges

☿ Objectivity and clarity of expression incorporate discipline and a cautious, systematic approach; often a good memory

♄ Conscious mind is stabilized by a practical sense of order and knowledge of tradition—a persistent, conscientious intellect

Mercury-Uranus Interchanges

☿ Independence and originality blend with mental and verbal ability—a quickness of mind that often jumps over details and goes to extremes

♅ A high-strung, inventive intellect makes new and unusual associations of ideas; impatient with others' slowness of mind and with formal education

Mercury-Neptune Interchanges

☿ Mental processes are turned toward universal themes and imaginative explorations

♆ The need to express one's perceptions and intelligence is guided by idealism—a highly sensitized, subtle intellect

Mercury-Pluto Interchanges

☿ An urge to penetrate to the core of experience underlies one's communications—an intensified, highly focused intellect

♇ A need to learn through intense, transformative, in-depth experiences, even if it means breaking taboos

Mercury-Ascendant Interchanges

Skill, dexterity, and intellectual qualities need to be expressed outwardly in many areas of life

Talking, making connections, and trying to understand are integral to one's mode of self-expression and entire approach to life

Aspects with Venus

The aspects with Venus primarily affect the capacity for conscious relationship with others, both in intimate one-to-one relations and in more general social relationships, as well as the ease with which one can experience emotional fulfillment in these relationships. In addition, Venus aspects reveal a lot about how easily one can express pleasure and how easily one can have his or her needs for pleasure satisfied. All the arts are also ruled by Venus, as well as various kinds of taste and social graces. How easily one can give and receive affection is clearly shown by Venus aspects, and the more harmonious aspects indicate open channels for giving and receiving in the ways indicated by the planets, signs, and houses involved.

However, it should be clearly stated that squares, oppositions, and various other challenging aspects with Venus do not necessarily mean that one is not loved or that one is incapable of feeling love. That is a misinterpretation of these interchanges. But the more dynamic angles involving Venus do usually reveal that one habitually blocks one's expression of love and keeps oneself from receiving it from others. Working on clarifying such blocks and fears and improving the flow of energy in that area can contribute substantially to greater pleasure and happiness.

Venus-Mars Interchanges

♀ Affections are expressed physically and dynamically; sometimes there is heightened eroticism

♂ One's need to feel pleasure and harmony blends with desire and action—often quite artistic; the ability to combine strength and grace, especially in physical activities like athletics

[The interaction between Venus and Mars has a major impact on our love relationships. The harmonious aspects between them aid the expression of each energy, whereas the challenging aspects, although perhaps symbolizing greater emotional and passionate intensity, are more troublesome in many cases. Often-times, with the challenging aspects, one can be impatient, ir-ritable, and changeable with those one cares about. In those cases, the person often gives "affection" and shows "caring" so abruptly and forcefully that it's not recognized as love and affection at all by the other person! Even if there is no major aspect between Venus and Mars, it is useful and highly illuminating to compare their relative compatibility by element.]

Venus-Jupiter Interchanges

♀ Love is expressed in an open, generous, and expansive man-ner, and a sense of beauty is often dominant in the character
♃ A liking for adventure and a concern for self-improvement color one's approach to relationships; can be excessive sen-suality and extravagance with money or emotional expression

Venus-Saturn Interchanges

♀ Expression of love is easier when one feels very secure and stable—steadies the affections through loyalty; great depth of love can be expressed if fears can be released
♄ Needs to feel close to another through shared effort, accepted responsibilities, and mutual commitment; hesitant to ex-press affection unless guarantees are present, and this unadventurous approach may lead to a rather dismal social life

Venus-Uranus Interchanges

♀ Feels a need to share with others one's sense of individual-ity, excitement, and freedom—electrifies the affections; can be insensitive and self-centered
♅ Needs to experiment with a unique variety of pleasures to feel completely satisfied—can be flirtatious; easily bored in relationships and dislikes possessiveness

[When the planet of relationship (Venus) blends with the planet of self-centered rebellion and independence (Uranus), problems can arise. See page 121 of *Astrology, Karma & Transformation* for much more detail on these aspects, which are often puzzling and challenging.]

Venus-Neptune Interchanges

♀ Yearns for a state of ideal love; lives in a dream of romantic, artistic, or spiritual bliss; nebulous fears or escapism can inhibit real relatedness
♆

Needs to express affections in order to experience a oneness with life, a complete merger with the whole—refines and sensitizes the affections

Venus-Pluto Interchanges

♀ A need to give of one's most profound emotions at the same time one is undergoing a thorough transformation and challenging social taboos
♇

Affections and tastes are colored by the urge to penetrate to the core of experience—intense, extreme feelings

Venus-Ascendant Interchanges

One's social and love involvements affect the entire approach to life

Artistic sense and refined tastes are integral to one's mode of self-expression

Aspects with Mars

Any aspect involving Mars makes a statement about power, physical and sexual energy, decisive action, leadership, pioneering courage in trying out new areas of experience, and areas of life wherein one may exert initiative. Patience is always difficult in areas where Mars is active, and yet in this physical world, patience is usually required to get maximum results from the impulsive, originating actions of Mars.

Mars-Jupiter Interchanges

♂ An expansive need for physical, sexual, or pioneering excitement, and an urge for adventurous action and accomplishment

♃ Desire and initiative focused toward improvement of self and toward broad, inspiring goals for improving life for others (often leadership in one's chosen field)

Mars-Saturn Interchanges

♂ Expression of assertive and instinctual energies needs to be structured and disciplined; patience helps one achieve one's goals

♄ One focuses physical, sexual, and leadership energy toward demanding goals and definite achievement

Mars-Uranus Interchanges

♂ One asserts oneself impatiently with originality and independence—often very rebellious; energized by a sense of freedom

♅ Strong need for unrestrained physical and sexual excitement; always wants new, exciting action in every sphere of life

Mars-Neptune Interchanges

♂ Has the ability to act on ideals and dreams and to actualize a distant vision; high ideals stimulate accomplishment

♆ Feels an urge to transcend the physical world and sexual desires, coupled with a constant flow of lively fantasies and often special talents which can appear "supernatural"

Mars-Pluto Interchanges

♂ An urge to transform situations and eliminate impediments through decisive (sometimes ruthless) actions

♀ Willpower is consciously directed toward total transmutation, reform, and use of concentrated power; wants to penetrate to the core of experience

Mars-Ascendant Interchanges

Self-assertive, pioneering, and aggressive urges need to be expressed outwardly

Physical, sexual, and leadership energies are integral to one's mode of self-expression

Aspects with Jupiter

Any aspect involving Jupiter bears examination since Jupiter expands whatever it touches. Jupiter can show where you try to improve things and develop them to their fullest, as well as to express those energies to their fullest, possibly at a very high level. Jupiter's expansiveness and pervasive optimism can, however, also lead to over-extending oneself in the areas indicated by aspect, signs, and houses, if moderation is not regularly observed. The generosity and positive attitude and broad, philosophical approach often shown by Jupiter can, at best, lend an aura of nobility and masterful accomplishment to those areas of life supported by Jupiter's upbeat energies.

In general, the Jupiter aspects involving one of the five personal planets or the Ascendant (or Midheaven) are the most important such aspects for everyone. However, Jupiter's interactions with the other planets, the guidelines for which follow, can be of great importance if Jupiter rules (or co-rules) the Ascendant, Sun Sign, or Moon Sign or is in some other way tied in closely to the major themes of a chart. Hence, if one of those three major factors is Sagittarius (or Pisces, which it co-rules with Neptune), all Jupiter aspects take on greater prominence.

Jupiter-Saturn Interchanges

(Especially important if Jupiter or Saturn rules a sign emphasized in your chart.)

♃ Urge toward a larger order is brought down to earth and stabilized— expands the ambitions

♄ One's urge to expand constantly interacts with one's need to retain the existing structure for safety

[Whether Saturn or Jupiter is stronger in a chart will have much to say about these energies' expression. The challenging aspects of Jupiter and Saturn are sometimes quite problematical in complicating the person's ability to work out his or her ambitions and long-range goals. Whereas the conjunction tends to be fairly harmonious and stimulates strong ambition in a focused way, the other dynamic aspects often manifest as a deep-down feeling that there is not enough work, money, or opportunity until one has over-extended oneself and finds that one in fact has too much to handle. Either feeling, that of having too much or too little, leaves the person frustrated. There is a profound need to learn contentment with working with what is at hand in the present.]

Jupiter-Uranus Interchanges
(Especially important if Jupiter or Uranus rules a sign emphasized in your chart.)

♃ Faith and large-scale future plans are electrified and expressed in an individualistic and unconventional way

♅ The need for change, experiment, and excitement is expansive and pervasive

Jupiter-Neptune Interchanges
(Especially important if Jupiter or Neptune rules a sign emphasized in your chart.)

♃ A pervasive need to experience oneness with something larger than one's own individual self and petty personal
♆ concerns

One believes in the reality of the intangible realm of experience, sometimes leading to an overactive imagination and a constant urge to escape or to a sense of meaningful inspiration

Jupiter-Pluto Interchanges
(Especially important if Jupiter or Pluto rules a sign emphasized in your chart.)

♃ A need to experience total rebirth stimulates the search for faith in a greater order in the universe

♇ Seeks to improve oneself through the power of transformative methods and pursuits

Jupiter-Ascendant Interchanges

Expansive, confident, and broad-minded qualities need to be expressed outwardly

Faith and optimism are integral to one's mode of self-expression and color one's entire approach to life

Aspects with Saturn

Any aspect with Saturn shows where energies are concentrated and where an especially serious approach is taken. Saturn's aspects reveal the ease with which one can handle limits: using power and authority through acceptable limits and proper channels, or feeling too limited to express oneself freely. If one limits oneself too much unnecessarily, then one might have to reorient the way one disciplines oneself.

In general, the Saturn aspects involving one of the five personal planets or the Ascendant or Midheaven are the most important such aspects for everyone.* However, Saturn's blendings with the other planets can be of great importance if Saturn rules or co-rules the Ascendant, Sun Sign, or Moon Sign or is in some other way tied in closely to the major themes of a chart. Hence, if one of these three major factors is Capricorn (or Aquarius, which it co-rules with Uranus), all Saturn aspects take on greater prominence.

Saturn-Uranus Interchanges
(Especially important if Saturn or Uranus rules a sign emphasized in your chart.)

♄ One feels the need to work toward original self-expression and to give practical form to one's unorthodox new ideas

♅ The need for change and excitement combines with the need for social approval—a way of working within a tradition is called for (perhaps a responsible and disciplined re-evaluation in the area indicated)

[These blendings can have a profound impact on one's overall attitudes. At best, they produce a creative combination of prac-

---

*See pages 76 to 79 in *Astrology, Karma & Transformation* for detailed explorations of Saturn in aspect to the personal planets. This material can augment the basic guidelines for these aspects in previous sections of this chapter.

ticality with progressive ideas and new methods of achievement. If not well integrated, moving from the old to the new is always difficult since the person wants freedom and excitement but won't let go of the past.]

Saturn-Neptune Interchanges
(Especially important if Saturn or Neptune rules a sign emphasized in your chart.)

♄ ♆ Disciplined effort is expended toward one's spiritual yearnings and ideals; the continual interaction between the world and the otherworldly can result in confusion and a lack of organization or in a practical grasp of subtle realities

One feels the urge to transcend a too-rigid physical structure and its uninspiring limitations; can infuse one's ambitions and commitments with idealism

Saturn-Pluto Interchanges
(Especially important if Saturn or Pluto rules a sign emphasized in your chart.)

♄ ♇ An urge toward total rebirth and transformation, which can lead to a deeper sense of inner security; a desire to work hard to leave behind the hauntings of the past

A compelling need to understand one's true priorities, desires, and motivations at an extremely deep level—often a profoundly intense ambition

Saturn-Ascendant Interchanges

Ambitious and responsible attitudes need to be expressed outwardly, and a serious, practical tone colors the entire approach to life

Disciplined energy and reliability are integral to one's mode of self-expression

Aspects to the Ascendant

Aspects to the Ascendant by any planet are invariably of great importance, since they color one's entire approach to and outlook on life.* It is very important, however, to consider the likely accuracy of the birth time before making any judgment about such an aspect. A change of approximately four minutes in the birth time can result in the Ascendant (and all the house cusps) being altered by one degree. Therefore, what may seem like a close aspect to the Ascendant may become more than 7° off from exact if the birth time is one-half hour in error.

However, since the impact of a planet being in close aspect to the Ascendant does result in that planet's qualities blending thoroughly with the expression of the Rising Sign's energy, one can use these aspects with the Ascendant as quite reliable indicators of how accurate the birth time is. For example, if a chart based on a specific birth time has any planet closely conjunct the Ascendant, but that planet's energy is not particularly in evidence in the personality, there is a strong likelihood that the birth time (or the standard time or daylight time or time zone used in calculating the chart) is wrong.

Uranus-Ascendant Interchanges

Independence and uniqueness need to be expressed outwardly, and an unpredictable, unorthodox approach to life is natural

Inventiveness, individualism, and a craving for the new and exciting are integral to one's mode of self-expression

Neptune-Ascendant Interchanges

Compassion, imagination, and/or spirituality need to be expressed outwardly and color one's entire approach to life; sensitizes the physical body to outside influences

---

*For additional guidelines for understanding the aspects to the Ascendant, see that section in Chapter 6 of this book.

Fantasies, dreams, and inspirations are integral to one's mode of self-expression

Pluto-Ascendant Interchanges

 Intensity, a deep privacy, and penetrating insights color the entire approach to life

Transformative and compulsive energies are integral to one's mode of self-expression—a strong willpower for better or worse

Aspects with the Outer Planets

Although all the important aspects with the outer planets have been mentioned already in this chapter, it seems appropriate in a book on interpretive guidelines to at least summarize their general meanings briefly. For a much more detailed treatment of the significance of the outer planets' aspects, including in-depth explorations of each outer planet's interchange with each personal planet, I refer the reader to Chapters 6 and 4 of *Astrology, Karma & Transformation.*

Aspects with Uranus ⛢

Uranus electrifies and speeds up whatever it touches. It induces spasmodic, sudden activity and rapid change. In any area of life, it prompts excitement and breaking of rules and traditions. It lends a certain instability to anything it touches, as well as a craving for excitement.

Aspects with Neptune ♆

Neptune refines and sensitizes whatever it touches. It can idealize, spiritualize, or merely deceive. In any area of life, it adds a touch of magic, imagination, or inspiration, whether or not the person is grounded enough in the practical world to utilize these energies effectively and healthfully.

Aspects with Pluto ♇

Pluto intensifies and energizes with willpower anything it touches. It adds a quality of depth and thoroughness, and the urge to eliminate all old and unnecessary patterns, habits, and activities. It lends an ability to remold the self through the use of will and mind power, and at best it reveals a great self-discipline and capacity for reform within and without. At worst, it is a ruthless, might-makes-right approach that can become compulsive in the area indicated.

CAUSE AND EFFECT

*Originally published in April, 1944. Excerpted from *Astrology, Science of Prediction* by Sidney K. Bennett, Wynn Publishing Co., Los Angeles, CA, 1945.

CHAPTER 9

GUIDELINES TO CHART SYNTHESIS

*Astrology has its beginning in a
remote sense of some great cosmic unity.*
—Goethe

Realistically, *synthesis* cannot be achieved merely through techniques of *analysis*, and "chart synthesis" ultimately cannot be taught, because direct perception of the unity and meaning of any birth chart can only come with experience and—to some extent—innate intuitive ability. Nevertheless, there are a few guidelines that could be extremely helpful to new and intermediate students of astrology which they rarely see mentioned in books. Being aware of such key guidelines can save students years of dead-end directions, worry-engendering habits, and frustrating confusion.

It is perhaps even more important today than ten or fifteen years ago to acknowledge and indeed to stress the importance of a wholistic view of the birth chart—an approach based on seeing all components of a chart as parts of a living whole. The computers which are increasingly used today not only for chart calculation but also for supposed "interpretation" erroneously lead many people to assume that large quantities of separate analytical components constitute a "chart interpretation." But achieving real synthesis and arriving at a wholistic vision of the chart is precisely what computers cannot do. Of course, trying to arrive at such a vision of the chart necessitates ways of synthesizing the diverse factors being interpreted. However, the whole is greater than the parts, and although students of astrology invariably must *begin* to approach synthesis through detailed analysis, the time must eventually come for experienced, capable practitioners when the analysis becomes immediate knowledge, and the knowledge—illuminated through interaction with the specific facts of the person's life—merges into a synthesized whole.

Achieving that level of ability is rare and requires considerable work, although some people do "catch" that knack much sooner than others. Arriving at that kind of wholistic view of the chart is an art, and, while many people learn the basics of the science of astrology, far fewer learn this art. Chart synthesis simply cannot be taught in books. The real aim of chart synthesis is to understand not the chart alone, but the *person*, and this involves tuning in on the major life themes of the person. The primary mode of synthesis is to learn to recognize those major themes of a birth chart which reflect the major themes of a person's life. We will discuss below how to recognize those themes.

Although, as mentioned above, real chart synthesis cannot be learned from books, a few have been published that lead the reader toward a wholistic, flexible, dynamic approach to chart interpretation.* First are many of the works by Dane Rudhyar, who pioneered the modern approach of a wholistic view of birth charts. Also, Charles Carter's *Essays on the Foundations of Astrology* (Theosophical Publishing House, Wheaton, IL) contains some rare gems on combinations of signs and other material

---

*No doubt there are other books than those mentioned here which contain significant material on chart synthesis. I encourage all students of astrology to read as widely as possible and to *experiment* with the interpretations in each book they read to see how accurate and revealing they are.

which can contribute to chart synthesis. Tracy Marks' *The Art of Chart Interpretation* (CRCS Publications, Sebastopol, CA) is one of the few books that systematically takes the reader through guided steps that aim toward ultimately synthesizing the major factors of the chart and ranking them in order of priority.

Also, my other books go quite far in describing many factors involved in chart synthesis. As one correspondent kindly wrote me, my descriptions in various books are "permeated with a sense of synthesis, a sense that *every* energy interacts with every other in some way." Specifically, *Astrology, Psychology & the Four Elements* contains a great deal of important material on evaluating the balance of the four elements, a procedure that is essential for chart synthesis. In addition, Chapter 7 of *The Jupiter-Saturn Conference Lectures* (soon to be retitled *New Insights in Modern Astrology*) is exclusively devoted to the subject of chart synthesis, as are various sections of my other books. Chapter 5 of *The Practice & Profession of Astrology* explains some important principles underlying chart synthesis. There is also a great deal of important material scattered throughout my books* on counseling issues and using astrology effectively with people. Much of that material bears directly on the subject of chart synthesis.

The structure and sequence of this book reflects what I see as the relative importance of the various chart factors, and to what degree each can be used and relied upon for accuracy. For example, emphasizing the elements at the start of this book simply reflects how they should likewise be emphasized at the start of any chart interpretation. And then, emphasizing the positions of the planets in the signs next reflects the fact that the planets' sign positions are the next most important factors in any chart.

---

*See the following works for specific material on astrological counseling, how to approach chart interpretation, astrology-psychology issues, etc.: Chapter 7 in *Astrology, Psychology & the Four Elements*; Chapter 12 in *Astrology, Karma & Transformation*; Chapter 5 in *Relationships & Life Cycles*; part of Chapter 4 in *The Jupiter-Saturn Conference Lectures* on psychological theory in relation to astrology; and various parts of *The Practice & Profession of Astrology*. (All available from CRCS Publications.)

Each planet is strongly "colored" or "toned" by the sign it is in, and that sign is invariably a *major* tone of that planet, and in fact usually the planet's dominant tone. However, other factors also tone that particular planet's expression, as the following explains.

Factors Toning Each Planetary Principle

Each planet represents a specific dimension of experience, and that dimension of experience is toned or colored by a myriad of factors. In other words, how will each dimension of experience (shown by the planets) be toned or colored in your life? When you begin to examine all the factors toning each planet, so many things must be taken into account that, in fact, you have to use considerable psychic energy to begin to *feel* them all at once. The analytical mind simply can't cope with such a variety and quantity of variables all at once, each of them having an effect in a slightly different degree.

The following factors all affect a particular planet and thus constitute the tones or colorations of a certain dimension of experience:

1) The planet's Sign. This is the fundamental energy wave and attunement of the planet in a particular chart, and it is symbolic of a dominant mode of expression of that planetary principle. Other factors modulate this basic attunement.

2) The planet's Subtone. This is the Sign position of the planet's dispositor, utilizing the ancient rulers only (e.g., a person who has Moon in Virgo and Mercury in Sagittarius is a person who has a Virgo Moon with a Sagittarian Subtone).

3) The planet's *close* Aspects. The major aspects, including all thirty-degree multiple angles, all noticeably color a planet's expression.

4) The planet's House position. For example, if a person's Venus is in the third house, it is similar to having a Mercury aspect to Venus, i.e., a Mercurian tone is added to the basic Venus attunement.

One could go on adding various minor factors, but that would unnecessarily complicate what is already a very complex picture. Eventually, one would wind up having every planet influenced or "toned" by every other astrological factor! At a certain profound level of unity and wholeness, this is of course true. But for the practical purpose of chart synthesis in order to better understand specific qualities, energies, abilities, and problems of an individual, one must focus within certain limitations and guidelines. One needs to focus on the major reliable factors, especially those that repeat.

As an example, let's consider a specific chart* and focus just on one planet. With the Moon in Sagittarius, there is a dominant Sagittarian tone to how this person *reacts* to all sorts of things and situations. The Moon principle is *reaction*—how do you react instinctively and spontaneously to anything? No matter what other factors are toning this person's Moon, there will always be some of that Sagittarian quality in the way he reacts to life's demands: bluntness, fiery defensiveness, broadmindedness, enthusiasm, tolerance, a need to link life's small events to larger issues, an urge to teach or to preach, and so on. Hence, the Sign position of the Moon is the dominant tone, but let us briefly consider the other factors that were just mentioned above.

The Subtone of the Moon: The Moon's subtone is Virgo since Jupiter, the ruling planet of Sagittarius, is in Virgo. So, this person is a particularly analytical Sagittarian Moon. Jupiter in Virgo is analyzing and trying to figure out why the lunar part of the self is so unwarrantedly optimistic, for Virgo can always find numerous problems! Virgo is square Sagittarius, after all. It does produce a very mental person when both of these signs are strongly energized. So, there is a Virgoan tone added to this person's Sagittarian Moon.

---

*See next page for complete chart.

Aspects with the Moon: First and most importantly, the Pisces Sun is exactly square the Moon. The Pisces sensitivity is always "toning" or coloring the more forceful and relatively insensitive Sagittarian Moon, while simultaneously the Moon's enthusiastic, optimistic qualities are constantly coloring the expression of the usually cautious, introverted Pisces Sun. Mars in Aquarius, sextiling the Moon closely, adds another coloration of experimentation and adventuresomeness to the Sagittarian Moon, stimulating further the urge to travel and liking for change and excitement. This orientation is further amplified by the close Uranus aspect to the Moon, another indicator of this person feeling comfortable

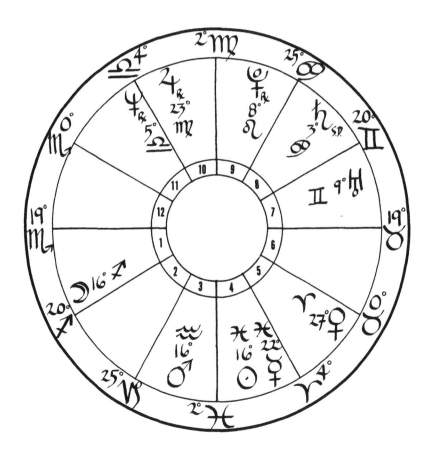

mainly when in the midst of variety, travel, learning, excitement, and change of all kinds. (Keep in mind that both Sun and Moon are mutable signs, both of which therefore crave variety and are unusually flexible in adapting to changes.)

These various tones affecting the Moon are so far adding up to give a fairly clear and very strong single message. However, when one looks at the House position of the Moon, there appears a bit more complexity. The Moon is in the Second House, where it is usually quite comfortable. (The Moon is traditionally exalted in Taurus, the Sign associated with the second house.) However, when a person has this Second House tone of stability, reluctance to change, attachment to routine pleasures, and stubbornness added to a Moon that is otherwise just the opposite of those qualities, the astrological counselor has plenty of substantial issues and complex qualities to discuss with the client. (I should not leave this subject without acknowledging that this person has generally made his living through teaching, including through workshops and seminars that required travel. He has even taught long workshops in foreign countries, excellently symbolized by a Sagittarian Moon in the Second House!)

Human beings are so complex that, if you begin to talk about "chart synthesis" or "chart interpretation," where is the end of it? Each planet is so interwoven with other factors and often incorporates such a complex of various tones and colorations that the astrology student, especially the beginner, often becomes extremely confused and discouraged. That is why the chart must always be related to specific issues, problems, decisions, and questions that the person is involved in. One needs to focus on what is important for the person in order not to get lost in endless possibilities. If one tries to do a "complete reading" for a person, there is no end to it; it is really an absolute impossibility. How could any of us ever sum up such a complex, infinite, and ever-changing mystery as a human being?

Understanding Themes in the Birth Chart

After considering the various dominant tones affecting the personal planets of a chart, one may notice one or several tones that seem especially dominant by being repeated over and over. Recognizing such pervasive tones is the first step toward recognizing *themes* in any chart. One effective method of further understanding themes in a chart is to combine the chief factors of the chart by using the "twelve letters of the astrological alphabet"* in all their combinations and seeing which combinations (or "interchanges") repeat significantly.

The astrological alphabet is basically as follows:

Letter 1: Aries, Mars & 1st House
Letter 2: Taurus, Venus & 2nd House
Letter 3: Gemini, Mercury & 3rd House
Letter 4: Cancer, Moon & 4th House
Letter 5: Leo, Sun & 5th House
Letter 6: Virgo, Mercury & 6th House
Letter 7: Libra, Venus & 7th House
Letter 8: Scorpio, Pluto & 8th House
Letter 9: Sagittarius, Jupiter & 9th House
Letter 10: Capricorn, Saturn & 10th House
Letter 11: Aquarius, Uranus & 11th House
Letter 12: Pisces, Neptune & 12th House

For example, if one's chart not only has Mars in Scorpio (an interchange between astrological letters 1 and 8, thus coloring or *toning* the expression of the Mars energy with a Pluto quality) but also includes a close Mars-Pluto aspect (another interchange of letters 1 and 8), there is a double emphasis on the same combination of energies; and hence, the expression of Mars

---

*I believe that Dr. Zipporah Dobyns (Ph.D., Psychology) was the first to popularize the concept of "12 letters of the astrological alphabet," a unifying concept which I found extremely helpful in simplifying chart interpretation and especially in teaching chart synthesis in my classes.

energy will be powerfully characterized by Plutonian qualities. If Mars is also in the 8th house or if Pluto is in the 1st house, this theme will be even more dominant.

Another example might help to explain this mode of synthetic analysis, especially for beginning and intermediate students of astrology. Suppose a person has Mercury in Capricorn; this person's attunement of the conscious mind will inevitably share some *fundamental* qualities with *all others* who have this Mercury placement. But suppose this particular person also has Saturn in close aspect to Mercury. This gives us two different emphases on the same theme: an interchange of astrological letters (or principles) 3 and 10 (or between 6 and 10 if the Virgoan dimension of Mercury seems strong for this person). With such a double emphasis on the same fundamental dynamic, we know that this individual will have a strong propensity toward handling exacting detail, toward a serious and practical mode of thinking, toward nervous tension, and toward working hard to develop certainty about their ideas. If this person has other factors in the birth-chart which also represent interchanges between these same principles (such as Mercury in the 10th house or Saturn in the 3rd or 6th house), there would be even greater dominance of this theme in the person's life; and the astrologer could therefore know with certainty that this would have to be one of the major things discussed during the consultation.

Another area of interpretation and chart synthesis which students of astrology find difficult is the entire question of *configurations* between many planets, involving a number of different aspects. Ultimately, only years of experience and practice will enable the student to overcome this seemingly insurmountable obstacle; for one must develop the ability to see configurations in a chart as a whole and to *blend* the meaning of all the planets involved in such complex combinations. However, many textbooks are so filled with abstract theory about various configurations (grand trine, T-square, grand cross, kite, etc.) that they make the whole process seem much more difficult than it really is. What is usually ignored is the fact that all those various factors and details simply symbolize facets of *one whole, living person.* And, in such configurations, there are two basic things to keep in mind which are much more important than the exact type of configuration involved:

A. Rather than focusing upon the type of configuration being considered (for example, a grand trine, yod, kite, etc.), one must primarily understand the meaning of the **planets** involved and their specific interchanges with other planets in that configuration. One is then able to blend these meanings in a way which accurately reflects how an individual actually *experiences* these energies. *Any* of the traditional configurations can be productive and creative, regardless of beliefs to the contrary, since they *all* represent *particularly intensified interactions* of the energies and principles symbolized by the planets involved. Secondarily, one should blend the energies of the **signs** involved in the configuration.

B. Most of all, one should focus one's attention on any **personal planet** (or the Ascendant) involved in a configuration, for that factor symbolizes the most immediate mode of expression for the energies of the *entire* configuration; and it reveals a dimension of the individual's being which is usually at least partially conscious and therefore has a particularly direct impact on his or her everyday experience. An individual will be able to *identify* with the meaning of a personal planet, and thus will be more able to understand and perhaps to modify the expression of that energy.

Finally, I have been urged to include in this book a simple, systematic *Outline of Chart Interpretation* which lists a sequence of steps that beginners might follow in trying to understand any chart. Although "chart synthesis" will not develop just from following a sequence of guidelines, beginning students of astrology do need to start somewhere with an intelligent step-by-step approach to interpretation. Therefore, I have adapted an Outline that I have used in many beginning astrology classes.

Following such a systematic approach does have its drawbacks; in reality, once a person has absorbed quite a lot of astrology, he or she will naturally tune into the major themes of that person's life and chart, replying to certain questions that a client may ask, and focusing on some chart factors while placing little emphasis on others. But that comes with experience. As I said above, people do need to start somewhere, and following this Outline will at least keep one oriented toward the *major* factors in a chart and keep one open to the wholistic nature of any chart and to the possibilities for chart synthesis.

The Outline includes a few chart factors and terms that are not explained in this book, but the reader can easily find the explanation for those terms in one of the astrological encyclopedias or major textbooks. It is outside the scope of this work to include all such traditional factors. An excellent explanation of virtually all astrological terminology is Nicholas DeVore's *Encyclopedia of Astrology,* an extremely intelligent and comprehensive work.

Outline of Chart Interpretation

I. The Chart as a Whole
  A. Preponderance & Deficiencies Shown by Planets'
      Positions
      1. By Sign Placement
          a) Element (Fire, Earth, Air & Water Signs)
          b) Quadruplicity (Cardinal, Fixed & Mutable
             Signs)
      2. By House Placement
          a) Angular, Succedent & Cadent
          b) Fire, Earth, Air & Water Houses
  B. Note the overall pattern of the chart; use your intui-
     tion to see the chart as a diagram of energy patterns.
     Note immediately any clusters of planets (a "stell-
     ium"), which strongly emphasize particular signs
     and houses.

II. The Main Components of the Chart Structure
  A. Using the Astrological Alphabet, note any major
     themes that emerge. Explore any tone that seems par-
     ticularly dominant.
  B. Dominant Aspect Patterns & Major Configurations
     (Grand Trine, T-Square, any Stellium, multiple
     aspects between a number of planets between two
     signs, etc.)

III. The "Lights"
  A. Compatibility of Sun & Moon by element
  B. The Sun
      1. Sign
      2. House
      3. Closest Aspect(s)
  C. The Moon
      1. Sign
      2. House
      3. Closest Aspect(s)

IV. The Angles (Birth time must be accurate to use these factors.)

    A. Note especially any conjunctions to the ASC or Midheaven; these planets are invariably powerful and magnified in intensity.

    B. The Ascendant
        1. Sign and compatibility with Sun Sign by element
        2. Closest Aspect(s)
        3. Position by Sign & House of the Ruling Planet of the ASC, as well as its close aspects

    C. The Midheaven
        1. Sign
        2. Closest Aspect(s)
        3. Position by Sign & House of the Ruling Planet of the MC

V. Traditional Techniques for Evaluation of Planets

    A. Planets weak or strong by sign placement (Planets in "Dignity," "Fall," "Exaltation," or "Detriment").

    B. Planets weak or strong by house placement (e.g., a planet in its own house, with the same letter of the astrological alphabet, is always especially strong).

    C. Note the Ruling Planet of the Sun Sign, its House, Sign & Aspects.

VI. Pivotal Components of Chart Structure

    A. Look to the closest square or opposition involving a personal planet, indicative of a primary challenge in life where the person has to strive and potentially can achieve a new awareness.

    B. Look to all conjunctions with personal planets, as well as other *close* aspects with the personal planets and their Signs and Houses.

    C. Any planet in the 1st House is very powerful: the closer to the ASC, the more powerful (including near the ASC on the 12th House side.)

    D. The House Position of Saturn is always important.

Books by the Author